The American Eskimo

Nancy J. Hofman & Cathy J. Flamholtz

ON THE FRONT COVER: Grand Champion "PR" Stevents Toybear Apollo, owned by Rosemary Stevens. *(Van Winkle & Associates photo)*

Frontispiece: Winterset Country Lace, owned by Nancy J. Hofman *(Doug Kaz photo)*

THE AMERICAN ESKIMO

ISBN 0-940269-04-X

© 1989 by OTR Publications

Printed in the United States of America

10 9 8 7 6 5 4 3 2

Library of Congress Cataloging-in-Publication Data

Hofman, Nancy J., 1935-
        The American Eskimo / by Nancy J. Hofman & Cathy J. Flamholtz
            p.   cm.
        Includes index.
        ISBN 0-940269-04-X
        1. Eskimo dogs.   I. Flamholtz, Cathy J.   II. Title
SF429.E8H64   1989
636.7'3--dc20   89-33045
                                                          CIP

Although the authors and publisher have extensively researched sources to ensure the accuracy and completeness of the information contained in this book, we assume no responsiblity for errors, inaccuracies, omissions or any inconsistency herein. Any slights of people or organizations are unintentional.

OTR PUBLICATIONS
P.O. Box 1243
Ft. Payne, Alabama 35967

Dedication

To the memory of Thomas Maxwell (1924-1986), the most influential man in the history of the breed. His dedication to the American Eskimo gave us both a history and a future.

To my family and friends who encouraged me to write this book and to all those who appreciate and love the American Eskimo breed.

Contents

Foreword

It is with great delight and true pleasure that I write this foreword to *The American Eskimo*. For many years, we have needed a comprehensive book on this breed. Often, Eskie owners have searched in vain for information about our breed. How wonderful it is that we now have a book of our very own.

Nancy Hofman is eminently qualified to author a book on the breed. Nancy acquired her first American Eskimo in 1971. Since that time, she has bred many Champions and Grand Champions. The first two Champion Eskies on the West Coast were owned by Nancy. In addition, she owned the first two Grand Champions in California. Nancy has served the breed well, both on the national and local levels. She was the Publicity Director for the National American Eskimo Dog Association and, for the past ten years, has served as President of the California American Eskimo Association. For the past fourteen years, she has written and edited the California American Eskimo Association's newsletter. Her articles, aimed at promoting the Eskie, have appeared in many dog magazines.

Nancy Hofman's dedication to the American Eskimo is unquestioned. Indeed, she has made this breed her life's work. She spends countless hours talking and corresponding with those interested in the breed. Those who know Nancy can attest to her honesty, integrity and dedication. It is Nancy who is always there to remind us to "keep the breed in mind first." In fact, I have never met anyone with a more thorough and extensive knowledge of the American Eskimo.

Nancy has an uncanny ability to get people involved in our breed. She has extended a hand to many new owners and they, in turn, have become dedicated American Eskimo enthusiasts. Whether it is helping to organize a dog show or talking a new owner, via telephone, through the whelping of that first litter, Nancy is always there when needed.

Those of us who know Nancy love her. We have great respect for her knowledge and expertise. The dog world needs more of her kind. This book is one more step in Nancy's tireless quest to promote the American Eskimo. I believe all Eskie owners will enjoy her book. *The American Eskimo* is truly a tribute to the breed we know as "The Dog Beautiful."

> *Rosemary Stevens*
> *President*
> *National American Eskimo Dog Association*

Igor ißt Cesar.

Mit feinem Fleisch in delikater Jelly.

Welche der a c h t feinen Sorten von Cesar wird Ihr kleiner Feinschmecker heute g e n i e ß e n?

Cesar. Für kleine Hunde mit großen Ansprüchen.

Looks like an American Eskimo, doesn't it? Yet, this European dog food advertisement features the popular white German Spitz. American Eskimo fanciers will note the amazing resemblance.

1

American Eskimo History

While the American Eskimo has been registered, in the United States, for well over seventy-five years, little has been written about the breed's historical background. Until recently, American Eskimo owners have only been interested in sharing their homes with their dogs. However, in the past few years, new fanciers have been attracted to the breed. They have begun to show their dogs in conformation and obedience competitions, and have undertaken serious breeding programs. In an effort to learn more about their favorite dogs, Eskie owners have begun to wonder about the breed's past.

When I first became involved with the American Eskimo, I discovered that little was known about the breed's history. I began to delve into books on dogs and, to my delight, I discovered many photos, both ancient and contemporary, which bore a striking resemblance to the Eskie. I culled through books which contained descriptions of these white dogs. To my amazement, they described a dog with the identical physical and temperamental characteristics possessed by our modern American Eskimo. As the evidence began to mount, it became obvious that our breed had a very long, proud and illustrious heritage. Yet, I knew that most Eskie owners were unfamiliar with this background.

The time has now come to fully document the American Eskimo's history. I hope that, by viewing the photos in this chapter and reading the quoted passages, American Eskimo owners can, at last, gain an appreciation of our breed's long association with man. By examining the findings of archaeologists and reviewing the works of historians, we can begin to piece together the long history of our white dogs. And, hopefully, by exploring the American Eskimo's background, we can come to understand the breed more fully and see how the many wonderful qualities we so admire developed.

WHAT'S IN A NAME?

Much of the confusion surrounding the history of the Eskie lies in the United Kennel Club's adoption of the name "American Eskimo." This appellation suggests the breed was developed entirely in the United States and was, perhaps, descended from dogs kept by the Eskimos. Nothing could be further from the truth. And yet, the U.K.C. should not be criticized for adopting this misnomer. Indeed, as we shall see, inaccurate names have always been applied to these dogs. As the record will reveal, there were sound, logical reasons for designating a new breed name, when the dogs were first registered in this country.

In Germany, since time immemorial, a great family of dogs existed. From the earliest days, these dogs, known to the Germans as the "Spitz," were to be found in many parts of the country. The same dogs lived in various localities, the only differences being in size and coat color.

Problems in correct identification of the dogs came only when they were exported from their German homeland. In the 1700's, in France, these German Spitz dogs were called "Loup-Loups." On the German border with Holland, the wolf-grey colored German Spitz was the most popular. The Dutch would adopt the breed, naming it the "Keeshond." In Italy, the small white Spitz would become fashionable. Here, it would be given the name "Volpino Italiani." The German Spitz even journeyed to far away Japan. There the breed would gain acceptance and become known as the "Japanese Spitz."

When the German Spitz was first exported to England, the dogs were called "Pomeranians." This was largely because the first dogs to appear were imported from the German province of Pomerania, located in what is now East Germany. However, Eskie fanciers should not jump to the conclusion that these dogs were one and the same as the breed now recognized as the Pomeranian. They were not toy dogs. Indeed, they were much larger, approximately the size of our current American Eskimo, and white was the desired color. Later, when the first very small Spitz dogs appeared in England, these larger white dogs were dubbed "Overweight Pomeranians" to differentiate them from their smaller cousins.

Yet, many dog writers did realize there was a difference and tried to clear up the confusion. In his 1906 work, *The New Book of the Dog,* Robert Leighton writes, "Long before the Pomeranian was common in Great Britain, this breed was to be met with in many parts of Europe, especially in Germany; and he was known under different names, according to his size and the locality in which he flourished. The title of Pomeranian is not admitted by the Germans at all, who claim this is one of their national breeds, and give it the general name of the German Spitz. This is the title assigned to it by Herr Karl Wolfsholz of Elberfeld in his work *Der Deutsche Spitz in Wort und Bilt,* published in 1906."

Today, in his homeland, the breed is still known as the German Spitz. Indeed, the Germans divide the breed into several varieties, based on size and color. These range from the tiny *Kleinspitz,* known in the United States as the Pomeranian, to the *Grosse Grau Wolfspitz,* better known in this country as the Keeshond. There are two sizes that are most interesting to the American Eskimo fancier, however. The first is the *Grosse Spitz,* or Large Spitz, which measures fifteen to nineteen inches. As Eskie fanciers will note, this dog corresponds in size to our male Standard American Eskimos. The other is the Middle-sized Spitz. At eleven to fourteen inches in height, this dog is the same size as our Miniature American Eskimo females. Photos carried in the German

Spitz club's publication, *Der Deutsche Spitz,* leave little doubt that we are talking about one and the same breed.

So we see that when the German Spitz has traveled to other countries, he has been received with open arms. Each country has embraced the breed and, in turn, made it their own. The United States is no exception. Here the legacy of the German Spitz lives on. But, as in other countries, he has been given his own unique and special name. In the United States, he is known as the American Eskimo.

BREED ORIGIN

The American Eskimo is a member of the large "Spitz" group, one of the most ancient types of dog. Most likely, our breed is descended from *canis familiaris palustris,* a dog which lived in the Neolithic, or Late Stone Age, of approximately 5,000 B.C. This early dog has been called the "dog of the lake settlements" or the "peatbog dog." Both names refer to locations where the skeletal remains of these dogs were discovered. Dogs of this type have been found in Germany, Switzerland and other Central European nations. Karl Ludwig Ruetimeyer, a noted German archaeologist, studied the skeletons located at these sites. He found that they closely resembled the breed now known as the German Spitz. His measurements of the skeletons revealed that the shoulder height was approximately eleven to fourteen inches, or roughly the size of our present Miniature American Eskimos. This size remained static for hundreds of years, but examination of later remains showed that, eventually, the height of the dogs increased somewhat.

We do not know precisely what role these dogs played in the life of early man. Many experts have theorized, however, that they served as guardians for human settlements. They believe that the dogs alerted their owners to the presence of wild animals. If so, we can see that watchdog duties were one of the earliest characteristics to develop in the Spitz breeds. Indeed, this may be one of the reasons why these dogs spread to so many parts of the world. Dogs resembling the modern Spitz breeds are found on tombs, coins, vases and statuary crafted by the ancient Egyptians, Greeks and Romans. Many of the dogs appearing on these artifacts were white in color and have an amazing resemblance to the American Eskimo.

THE 1500's

Dogs of the Spitz type became very popular in Germany. In fact, the word "Spitz," meaning "sharp point," is of German derivation. The first documented recording of the term "Spitz" was made by Count Eberhard zu Sayne, in 1540. Count zu Sayne was a feudal land baron, who made his home in Germany's Rhine Valley. His holdings consisted of thousands of acres of land, very rich in game. Here, Count zu Sayne and his friends indulged in splendid hunts. There is evidence to suggest that feudal lords, like Count zu Sayne, may

5

have presented Spitz dogs to their tenants. In the 1951 German book, *Dogs and Dog Care*, Ulrich Klever writes, "Straying and chasing game are things he does not know, because in comparison with his master's house and property, nothing is of any importance to him. When the hunting lords gave their tenants a Spitz, this was calculated generosity. They knew full well that a Spitz never chased game, no matter how rich a preserve he might have lived in."

Apparently, it was the habit among Count zu Sayne's servants to condemn those they did not like by calling them *Spitzhunds*. Perhaps the Count admired Spitz dogs, or he may just have wanted to insure harmony. At any rate, he issued an edict prohibiting the derogatory use of the word.

We also find the term "Spitz" in Geman dictionaries from the 1500's. Some early German fiction writers, from this period, mentioned the Spitz, portraying him as a valiant defender of the home. It seems safe, therefore, to conclude that the Spitz was well known in Germany during this period.

THE 1700's

The popularity of the Spitz, particularly in Germany, continued to grow. By the 1700's, the German Spitz was one of the most commonly seen dogs in the country. Germany had not yet become an industrial might. Instead, most citizens relied on agriculture for their living. In some sections of the country, nobility ruled over vast estates, with labor provided by peasants, who were responsible to the feudal lord. In other areas, people owned their own small plots of land.

The German Spitz became the cherished dog of the common man. On the farm, he was esteemed as a multifaceted, all-around watchdog *par excellence*. When the peasant was at work his Spitz would stay by the door, protecting the home. The owners could go about their daily tasks, secure in the knowledge that no stranger would be permitted on their property.

The Spitz was especially appreciated by the woman of the house. It was she who often attended to the vegetable garden, which provided food for the family. Yet, it was also her responsibility to watch over the children who were not yet old enough to work. Very often, it was one of the family's Spitz dogs who came to her aid. The baby might be placed on a blanket, at the edge of the garden plot, while mom attended to the planting, weeding and harvesting. Beside the child, lay the faithful Spitz dog. He served as the youngster's playmate, ever ready to bark should the child cry or a stranger approach. From the earliest years of a German child's life, therefore, the Spitz would become his best friend and loyal playmate.

The dog was equally valuable, however, to the man of the house. When the goods produced on the farm were taken to town for sale, one of the Spitz dogs always accompanied the cargo. Riding beside his master, in the wagon, the dog assured that no one would steal any of the produce. The Spitz was especially prized in the wine growing districts of Germany. William Ledbetter, in an article entitled, "Notes on the Origin and Development of the German Spitz," recalls the days when vintners brought their wine to town.

"Under the coach seat or behind the wine keg always lay the family's Spitz, watchfully observing the unfamilar surroundings. After business had been transacted and the wine had been brought down into the cellars of the restaurants, the wine producer celebrated with his patrons. In the evening, after the wine producer had left the city and was approaching his home area, it usually occurred that he fell asleep on the seat of his coach. The horse, of course, knew the way back to his stall—and the Spitz? He had control over *everything:* the farmer, the horse, the wagon, and above all, the farmer's wallet!!! No one dared to approach his master!"

The Spitz was equally popular in the coastal regions of Germany. Boats, engaged in fishing and trade, plied the Baltic Sea. Most took Spitz dogs with them, to protect their goods. When the boats docked, the men went ashore. Remaining behind were the Spitz dogs, who prevented any strangers from boarding. These seafaring Germans traded with the Scandinavians to the north,

The German Spitz was esteemed as a guardian of home and property. When the family went to town, it was the dog's duty to protect the wagon and cargo. This rare engraving, by an unknown German artist, shows both a black and a white Spitz at work.

Thomas Gainsborough's paintings give us a vivid portrait of what the dogs imported into England, in the 1700's looked like.

and the rest of Europe to the south and west. The dogs were admired in the many ports where German ships docked, and it seems likely that there developed a lively trade in Spitz dogs.

As we have seen, the German Spitz came in several different colors. Indeed, many regions of Germany seem to have had their own particular preferences as to color and size. The larger Black Spitz was said to be bred primarily in the Baden-Württemberg province. It is also reported that the Black Spitz was well known in Swabia, Stuttgart, Heidelberg, Heilbronn and Mannheim. In some of these locations, the dogs were referred to as "Spitzer." At other times, they took on the name of their location, and were called, for example, "Mannheimer Spitz."

In other regions of Germany, there could be found a wolf-colored Spitz. This gray colored variety was particularly prized in the areas adjacent to the Netherlands. In later years, the breed would be taken over, in part, by Dutch owners. They would give the breed the name of "Keeshond."

The German Spitz was sometimes also known by the work he did. Thus, dogs who aided German wine growers, were referred to as the *Weinberg Spitz* or "Vinyard Spitz." To this day, statues can be seen in Stuttgart and Bochum, which pay hommage to these vigilant guardians of the field.

What of the White Spitz? Various sources tell us that these dogs were popular in several different locations. All seem to agree, however, that the province of Pomerania was the home of many superb White Spitz. Those found in this area came in a variety of sizes. White Spitz from this region became popular in England. There, they became known as Pomeranians, although the Germans did not approve of this title. However, as we said, the Pomeranians of that day were far closer, in type, to our American Eskimo than to the toy breed, which today bears the Pomeranian name.

By the mid-1700's, the White Spitz had become the darling of British society. Credit for the breed's popularity must go to Queen Charlotte. The Queen was born in the German province of Mecklenberg and retained pleasant memories of the Spitz dogs she had known there.

Although erroneously called "Pomeranians," the white Spitz that were imported from Germany were really the size of our current American Eskimos.

She acquired several White Spitz, from Pomerania. In fact, it may have been Queen Charlotte who first officially introduced the name "Pomeranian" to England. Suddenly, the White Spitz became a very fashionable dog and everyone in Great Britain wanted to own a dog just like the Queen's. So popular did the dogs become that they had to be protected, when taken out, lest they be stolen. The Spitz, in Queen Charlotte's time, weighed about twenty to thirty pounds, and white was the most sought after color.

British dog lovers took great pride in displaying their White Spitz dogs. That these dogs were appreciated and valued is without question, for their owners had portraits of themselves, with their pets, painted by the most famous artists of the day. We can tell much about the dogs from the paintings of prominent artists of the period. Most notable among these are the works of Thomas Gainsborough (1728-1788).

THE 1800's

By the 1800's, British cynologists were writing about the White Spitz. Mention is made of the breed in *Cynographia Britannica,* published in 1800. In this early book, Sydenham Edwards describes the appearance of the "Pomeranian or Fox-Dog." He says that the dogs are about eighteen inches high, or roughly the size of our Standard American Eskimos. The ears are described as erect. The head is broad at the back and narrowing to the muzzle and the tail "large and bushy, curled in a ring on the rump." What attracted Mr.

Edwards attention most, however, was the ruff about the neck. "There is a peculiarity in his coat: his hair, particularly the ruff around his neck...is simply a semi-circle which...gives him a very beautiful appearance."

In the 1803 book, *Sportsman's Cabinet,* Taplin writes of this breed. "In England he is much more familiarly known as the fox-dog, and this may have originally proceeded from his having much affinity to that animal about the head." He goes on to describe the dogs seen at that time, in England, as standing about eighteen to twenty inches tall. He also tells us that "the dog...is distinguished by his long, thick and rather upright coat, forming a most tremendous ruff about his neck, but short and smooth on the head and ears....the head broad towards the neck, and narrowing to the muzzle; ears short, pointed, and erect; nose and eyes mostly black; the tail large, bushy, and invariably curled in a ring upon the back." On color, Taplin tells us, "They are mostly of a pale yellow or cream colour, and lighter on the lower parts. Some are white, some few are black."

In 1840, Sir William Jardine edited a mammoth encyclopedia of natural history called the *Naturalist's Library.* Volume Ten of the work, penned by Lt. Col. Charles Hamilton, was devoted entirely to dogs. According to Hamilton, the dogs known in England as Pomeranians, were the same dogs commonly seen as watchdogs on German farms. He also shows the new preference in color. The majority of the dogs seem in England were, according to Hamilton, white or buff in color.

One of the most noted of early British dog writers and judges was J.H. Walsh, who wrote under the pseudonym of "Stonehenge." In 1859, he wrote

"Charley" was a big winner in the English show rings of the 1880's. He stood sixteen inches tall and weighed eighteen pounds.

10

of the Spitz: "This cheerful little dog is extremely common in the continent of Europe...Until lately it was rare in England, but within the last twenty years has become very common as a house-dog."

In his 1878 book, Stonehenge comments "...he is always cheerful in the house, generally free from smell wither of coat or breath, and readily taught to be cleanly in his habits. He has not the fondness for game...and on that account is more suited to be a ladies' pet...From these peculiarities, it may be gathered that he is quite up to the average in his fitness to fill the position of companion."

In still another book Stonehenge tells us: "This pretty little dog is now very common in this country as a ladies' pet, his pretty white coat and lively manners rendering him a general favourite...He has one advantage, which is, that his coat, though long and rough, seldom becomes offensive."

The trend toward white dogs continued. The main objective in England was to breed a dog of pure white color. Rev. Thomas Pearce, who wrote under the pen name of "Idstone," tells us that, in 1872, color should be "a cold, flake-white" although it "frequently comes creamy."

In his 1881 book, *British Dogs,* Hugh Dalziel reiterates this belief, calling for a "pure flake-white" color and telling us that colored patches and fawn markings are objectionable. In addition, Dalziel first reports on instances of snow nose. He says that he has seen black noses fade to a brown or flesh color, when the dogs were exposed to heat, or allowed to "frequent the hearth."

Perhaps the most clear information on the Spitz, during this period, comes from the famous two volume work by Vero Shaw. *The Illustrated Book of the Dog* was written in 1870-1881. For the first time someone attempts to pen an early standard of the breed. The following is Shaw's description:

Skull-Wide and flat and foxy-looking, tapering towards the muzzle, which is very fine.

Jaws-Rather wide at base, but snipy towards nose.

Ears-Fine and pricked.

Eyes-Dark, not too full, and almond-shaped.

Chest-Rather wide.

Body-Short and cobby-looking.

Legs-Stout, and placed well under the body.

Feet-Round and small.

Coat-Rather coarse, and very dense all over the body, especially on the lower side of the neck. It is long all over the body, but short on the head, with some feather on the forelegs.

Tail-Bushy, and curled over the back.

Colour-White or black. As stated before, some permit lemon or other shades, but the two former are certainly by far the most preferable. Parti-colored dogs are much objected to.

General appear-ance-An active, sharp-witted dog, capable of enduring fatigue, and giving every indication of hardiness and activity.

Originally the darling of English nobility, the White Spitz continued to attract attention. By the late 1800's, he seems to have been beloved by both the

commoner and the aristo-
crat. An 1883 letter, which
appeared in the British
publication, *The Stock-
keeper,* spoke about the
breed's intelligence. It re-
counted the story of Mr.
George Nash, owner of the
Alexandra Hotel, and his
pet bitch *Floss.* No doubt,
the description of Floss'
prowess, as a keen-eared
watchdog, will have a
familiar ring to current
Eskie owners.

"This hotel is
provided...with bells to
each room for the purpose
of calling the attention of
the waiters, each bell having a different sound. There
is also an ordinary door-
bell, which is rung by a
handle at the front entrance
of the hotel, this bell being

A famous German opera star and her white Spitz.

similar in all respects to the others, saving a slight difference in tone, and is
fixed on the same board as the others. Now, persons calling at the hotel for
refreshments may ring as often as they please at any of the inside bells, but
Floss will not take the slightest notice of them, but let anyone ring the door-bell,
and though she be to all appearances asleep before the kitchen fire, which is at
the opposite side of the house to the front door, Floss will jump up and rush to
this door, barking all the while, as if she would clear the house in a minute; and
until she is perfectly satisfied that there is nothing wrong she will not return to
her warm quarters.

"What is still more remarkable is, that she can distinguish the sound of
the door-bell even when one of the other bells is ringing at the same time. Floss
is about six years old, but has only been at this hotel for twelve months, and her
peculiar qualification was only noticed by her owner a few weeks ago, since
which time the poor Floss has been repeatedly roused from her quiet slumbers
by persons desiring to test the accuracy of the...statements."

The story of the Pomeranian, which was in fact simply the German
White Spitz, was to change dramatically in England. With the ascent of the
beloved monarch, Queen Victoria, the breed was to be changed forever. The
Queen was an avid dog lover, who owned more that fifteen different breeds, and
her canine companions were always at her side. On a trip to Florence, Italy, in

12

1888, she returned with a Pomeranian named "Marco." He quickly became one of the Queen's favorites. Marco was a departure from the Poms generally seen at that time in England. At twelve pounds, he was considerably smaller than the twenty to thirty pound dogs that were the norm. His deep red sable coat color also distinguished him from the Poms commonly seen in England. Marco was exhibited at several London dog shows. Imagine competing against dogs owned by the Queen!

Once again, British royalty set breed style. When it was known that Queen Victoria preferred the small Pomeranians, they quickly gained favor. The era of the small Pomeranian, the forerunner of the toy breed we know today, had begun. This also signaled the decline of the old style Pomeranian in England.

THE WHITE SPITZ IN THE U.S.

We do not know precisely when the first German White Spitz arrived in this country. From examining the evidence, however, it seems that the breed, which would subsequently be called the American Eskimo, has been here for many, many years. It appears that the first of these dogs made an appearance well before the turn of the twentieth century.

In the 1879 British work, *The Illustrated Book of the Dog*, celebrated writer Vero Shaw acknowledges the presence of the breed in the United States. "This breed is fairly popular in America under the title of Spitz dog, and we have seen a very good specimen imported into this country by a lady who had visited the United States."

These miniature white German Spitz were born in 1931

13

It is most likely that the breed first arrived in this country with German settlers. It is also equally possible that visitors to England were attracted to Queen Charlotte's favorite dog and purchased specimens to bring back to this country. Canadian Eskie fancier Brian Webb visited the Franklin D. Roosevelt home and library in Hyde Park, New York. To his amazement, he found a photo of the three year old future president, with a White Spitz dog, astride a mule. The photo was dated 1885.

In his *The Dog Book,* published in 1905, American author and judge James Watson speaks of the White Spitz, which he calls "Large Pomeranians." He writes, "It is so seldom that we see any of these large Pomeranians at the present time that it is unnecessary to say more about them and a good idea of what they were a century ago is shown in the Gainsborough painting of Mrs. Robinson."

A 1919 issue of the *National Geographic Magazine* discusses the Spitz. It tells us that "Thirty or forty years ago it was popular in this country...." This would mean that the Spitz was well known in approximately 1879-1889. Describing the breed, the article says:

"The true spitz is a dog weighing about 25 to 30 pounds, and the best dogs are white or cream-color...They are bright, fascinating, pretty dogs; but it must in candor be said they are very "choicy" in making friends and very ready to repel with sharp teeth any unwelcome advances by dogs or humans they don't know. They are apt to be a real responsibility to the owner on this account...."

A very rare photo from 1934. Two year old Ray Vernimme poses with his friend Beauty. Mr. Vernimme is now a licensed Eskie judge.

THE WHITE SPITZ AND THE UNITED KENNEL CLUB

As we have seen, the White Spitz appears to have been popular, at the turn of the century, in this country. While many people owned dogs of this breed, however, there was no registering body which officially recognized the breed. We do not know how many people seriously breed the White Spitz.

One couple, however, did take a special interest in the White Spitz. Mr. and Mrs. F. M. Hall deserve the gratitude of all Eskie owners, for their love and dedication to the breed. These pioneers had been breeding the White Spitz for many years. They had purposely sought out dogs to supplement their breeding program, taking special care to obtain dogs from non-related stock. They also maintained their own pedigrees, which showed dogs of three generations or more, of their own breeding. Reportedly, the dogs in their kennels ranged between twenty and forty pounds in weight.

The United Kennel Club had been formed in 1898, by Mr. C. Z. Bennet. In 1913, the Halls approached Mr. Bennet, to discuss their White Spitz. They expressed their great desire to have the breed recognized and registered by the U.K.C. Mr. Bennet was receptive.

During the meeting, much attention was paid to the name of the breed. The Halls were not at all pleased with the appellation "Spitz." Not being German, they did not know what the word meant. They turned to the dictionary, but were unable to discover the word's meaning.

There may also have been several other reasons for deviating from the common "Spitz" label. In truth, this general and rather generic term was sometimes applied, haphazardly, to many dogs who bore little resemblance to the White German Spitz. Indeed, it seems that many mongrel dogs were sold under the label "Spitz." This was apt to cause confusion and to undermine the efforts of breeders producing dogs from a purebred bloodline. To this day, this attitude sometimes prevails. Therefore, American Eskimo owners have always been very firm in their demand that the breed be called something other than simply a "Spitz."

We must also remember that, when the Halls approached Mr. Bennet, the political situation in the world was rather tense. In 1913, the world was poised on the brink of the first great world war. Sentiment against German breeds, in the next few years, would build. Dachshunds, which had previously enjoyed great popularity, went into a steady decline during the war years. When introduced to Great Britain, the German Shepherd would be given a new name, the Alsatian, to distance the breed from its German heritage. Anti-German sentiment was at an all time high and some Americans, eager to avoid discrimination, denied their German lineage.

The American Eskimo has long been a family favorite in this country. Connie Jankowski can recall stories that her father and grandfather told of their Eskies. This photo, from 1940, shows "Lindy" with Connie's cousin, Diane.

This attitude resurfaced again during World War II. During the Second World War, dogs were occasionally auctioned off to raise money for the war bond drive. A story is told of such an auction, held in California. The breeds offered on the auction block had each been commanding several thousand dollars for the war effort. However, the mood changed dramatically when a Dachshund was brought before the people. There was not one bid and soon the crowd was yelling in anger, "Get that Nazi dog off the stage."

Thus, the political climate may well have played a part in the name change of the White Spitz. At the time, it may have been in the breed's best interest not to have it marked by an association with its German homeland.

How, then, did the name "American Eskimo" come to be associated with the breed? Once again, we must look to those breed pioneers, the Halls. They had named their kennel of White Spitz, the American Eskimo Kennel. It seemed an appropriate name for the breed which did, in some ways, resemble the dogs of the Eskimos that were, during that period, being introduced to this country. It was decided that the White German Spitz would, in the United States, be henceforth known as the American Eskimo.

BREED PROGRESS

In the years immediately following recognition and registration by the United Kennel Club, breed progress was slow. The U.K.C. is now the second largest registering body, but in those early years, many people did not yet know of its existence. Around the country, dogs continued to be bred and sold under the name of "Spitz." In books and articles from this period, most refer to the breed by this simple name.

Stories about the loyalty of these dogs captured the hearts of many people and earned the breed many loyal admirers. In 1944, the *New York Herald Tribune* ran the amazing story of one White Spitz who may have been a little too friendly for his own good.

"Six-and-one-half years is a long time in a dog's life. But exactly what happened to Junior, a little white Spitz, in the six-and-one-half years he was absent from his Brooklyn home probably will never be known. One thing is certain: Nothing was able to erase from his canine soul the memory of that home.

It is a one-family house at 1475 Carroll St., where live Mr. and Mrs. Albert A. Weinstein, and their two daughters, Jean and Phoebe.

Junior came to this household nine years ago when he was a puppy. Phoebe was eleven then and Junior would follow her to school. One afternoon in 1937, Phoebe and Junior were playing on the sidewalk when an automobile came by. The driver opened the door and whistled. Junior, whose fluffy white tail became a semaphore of happiness at any kind of attention, bounded into the car and was gone.

For a long time the Weinsteins ran advertisements in newspapers, promising rewards for the return of Junior or even for information about him. Many Spitzes were brought to their door but none was Junior.

One day recently Mrs. Weinstein was sitting on the front steps. She saw a dog limping up the street. His coat was dirty and full of burrs. He paused, sniffed a moment and resolutely came up the walk. He whined once and fell at her feet, revealing bloody paws worn almost to the bone from the rough pavements. The dog perked up somewhat after she fed him, and he responded to "Junior." Mrs. Weinstein then picked the burrs from his long hair and put him in the bathtub. Soap and water revealed the silken sheen of his coat, and Mrs.

Weinstein noted the two tiny patches of black hair near his left eye and on his nose. The Junior of six-and-one-half years ago was similarly marked.

As soon as he was dry Junior made a dash for an open door, then trotted up and down the block, sniffing at each child he passed, evidently hunting for Phoebe, the little girl he usedto follow to school.

When Phoebe finally did come home a ball of white shot around a corner of the houseinto her arms. A red tongue laved her face with kisses."

Is it any wonder the American Eskimo, often still called the Spitz, won the hearts of so many owners? Numerous accounts of the breed can be found in dog books from the 1920's to the 1940's. All describe a white dog, medium in size, with a tail curled over the back. Without exception, all tell of a dog incredibly loyal to those he loves.

STAR PERFORMERS

While the breed continued to rank high as a watchdog and companion, they also gained a reputation for being super-intelligent. Many were seen in traveling circuses and rodeos. The Barnum and Bailey Circus maintained a troupe of traveling Eskie performers. Crowds cheered as the white dogs leaped on to the backs of horses and balanced precariously on tighropes. But, the dogs also performed in less prominent groups.

Current American Eskimo fanciers, Dean and Jean McCroskie, tell of their introduction to the breed. "In 1956, our Mother went with us to the White Horse Ranch, near Naper, Nebraska. This was a summer camp for young people interested in learning circus type acts. While there, our Mother bought

Professional entertainers Dean McCroskie, with McCroskie's Mike, and Jean McCroskie, with Spike the Houdini.

us two white horses and our first two snow white American Eskimo puppies.

"These miniature male puppies were littermates. We named one McCroskie's Mike. The other...was Spike the Houdini. Their sire was Clipper ...and their dam was Cindy..."

White Horse Ranch was founded in the 1930's by Mr. Caleb R. Thompson.

'PR' McCroskie's Sandy, a Standard female, takes her babies for a stroll.

On his 2,700 acre spread, Mr. Thompson trained animals for circus acts. The white animals were his favorites. He developed a breed of white horses, noted for their trainability. These were sold to circus folk, show people and movie producers. Accompanying the white horses, were White Spitz dogs. Personally trained by Mr. Thompson, these dogs learned an amazing repertoire of tricks.

Mr. Thompson trained many youngsters in the art of performing. "He and a group of his students toured the U.S. and Canada during the 1940's and 1950's with trick horses and trick Spitz dogs, plus a few other trained white animals," the McCroskies tell us.

Caleb Thompson was not aware that the White Spitz could be registered with the United Kennel Club. To ensure the preservation of his superlative performers, he registered the dogs himself. He used the White Horse Ranch designation and the first dogs purchased by the McCroskies bore the W.H.R. prefix, followed by a registration number. It was only when Dean and Jean McCroskie told him, that he became aware of the U.K.C. "He was glad we had registered Mike and Spike with the U.K.C." Dean and Jean recall.

The story of Mr. Thompson's success with the white dogs may have inspired others to use the breed in their acts. "In 1957 and 1958, we studied under...Mr. Bernard R. Baranoski." Nicknamed "Pinky Barns," for the pink chaps he wore, Mr. Baranoski conducted the Famous 101 Ranch Shows. He was the 1924 all-round champion cowboy and an accomplished trick roper and bull whip artist. He was also a sought after pony, horse and dog trainer. Photos of him can be seen, today, in the Circus Hall of Fame. "In 1965, he wrote us," the McCroskies say, "and said he was using four standard and one miniature American Eskimos in his act. This was Pinkey's breed of dog."

Today, twin sisters, Dean and Jean McCroskie, carry on this performing tradition. And their dog of choice? The American Eskimo, of course. Currently,

18

These born hams are McCroskie's Mike, Spike the Houdini and Spike's son, 'PR' Twins White Chieftain.

their act includes "PR" Twins' Klondike King and his son, "PR" Twins' Husky Stuff. "The keys we have found to making a dog act are: First, some well-bred American Eskimos, and second, patience, practice and consistency. When we see a group of well-behaved trick dogs, doing an act together, we know it's no accident....Anything is possible with the American Eskimo!...We can say from experience that the American Eskimo is a tough act to follow and we want to keep it that way."

THE MODERN AGE

When we look at the state of the breed today we can see that remarkable progress has been made. Most people now realize that the proper breed name is the "American Eskimo" and that the dogs are registered with the United Kennel Club.

As we have seen, for many years the Eskie was thought of primarily as a pet and companion. In the 1960's fanciers began to band together to seriously improve the breed. They became interested in showing their dogs in conformation and obedience. On November 1, 1969, a group of dedicated fanciers met in DeSota, Missouri, to form the National American Eskimo Association. Later, the name would be changed to the National American Eskimo Dog Association. Forty three people attended this meeting, including Mr. and Mrs. Thomas Maxwell, of Davison, Michigan. Thomas Maxwell (1924-1986) would prove to be an untiring promoter of the breed. Serving as president of the National Club, for many years, he did much to help the organization of state Eskie

The famous Ch. Maxwell's Gidget, owned by Tom & Ruth Maxwell, was the world's first Champion American Eskimo.

19

clubs. He and his dogs appeared on television, and helped to introduce many people to the breed. His first American Eskimo, Maxwell's Gidget, became the very first breed champion. His miniature, Ch. "PR" Maxwell's Zsa Zsa was the first miniature female to earn the championship title. These were only the first of many Maxwell owned champions, including three Grand Champions and one National Grand Champion. Tom Maxwell traveled extensively, showing and judging Eskies. He took particular pride in helping newcomers to the breed.

The late Thomas Maxwell, who devoted his life to the breed.

After shows, his motel room became a traditional gathering place for anyone wanting to "talk Eskies." American Eskimo fanciers owe him a debt of gratitude for helping our breed.

Much progress has been made since the formation of the National Club. Many new people have joined the ranks of Eskie owners and have taken an active interest in the betterment of the breed. The number of state American Eskimo Clubs has grown. Currently, there are several clubs in California, two in Texas and others in Colorado, Indiana, Ohio, New England, Michigan, Nevada, Oklahoma and Wisconsin. Hopefully, these clubs will continue to grow and be joined by others, in new states.

Indeed, the American Eskimo has finally come into his own. From the dogs of Stone Age man to the valued watchdog of German farms, the American Eskimo has become accepted in the United States. He is still appreciated as a superb watchdog, but he is now also known as an animated show dog and an enthusiastic obedience performer. Current Eskie owners can point with pride to our breed's long and illustrious history. We find, in the American Eskimo, a dog who has always been esteemed as a partner to man.

20

2

The American Eskimo — A Family Dog

The American Eskimo is a family dog *par excellence,* as anyone who shares his home with one of the breed can attest. "The Dog Beautiful," as the Eskie has been christened, richly deserves praise for his devotion and loyalty. A proud, spirited and lovable animal, he lives to please and protect his family. And yet, despite his many laudable qualities, this is not the ideal breed for everyone. Those who want a yard dog, who will be happy left to his own devices, had best search for another breed or be prepared to provide their dog with another canine companion. The Eskie is not for the weak willed owner, either. This breed is assertive and determined and, if you allow it, will manipulate and dominate you. For those up to the challenge of Eskie ownership, however, the rewards are many. They will find, in the American Eskimo, a whimsical clownish spirit. Eskies can be wonderfully mischievous, bouncy, curious and always lively. They are also very, very expressive. Coupled with a sensitive and affectionate nature, the Eskie has an uncanny ability to understand people.

We hope, in this chapter, to honestly discuss the American Eskimo character. It's true that the Eskie attracts attention wherever he goes. And why not? This natural breed is extremely beautiful. In fact, many owners obtain their first dog strictly because of the breed's looks. Time is best spent, however, getting to know the dog beneath that glorious white coat. The true beauty of the American Eskimo lies not in his flashy looks, but in his sterling character.

All those considering obtaining an Eskie, must fully understand the breed's long guardian tradition. For centuries, the breed we know as the American Eskimo has been bred specifically to guard his family and their property. By his very nature, the Eskie is an instinctive and territorial watchdog. He is incorruptible in his mission to protect his family and will not be tempted by tidbits proferred by a stranger. Nothing can convince him to abandon his duties. An American Eskimo bonds so closely, with his family, that he considers both them and their property as belonging to him. In his mind, they are "his" and must be defended at all costs.

These guardian qualities lend the Eskie a reserved and aloof attitude with strangers. Most Eskies simply won't approach much less lavish attention on outsiders. The breed is apt to be extremely mistrustful of newcomers. For this reason, socializing your Eskie is imperative. If you have frequent, regular visitors, take the time to introduce them to your American Eskimo. Once he understands that their visits are not cause for alarm, he will accept them as part of his routine. Eskie puppies should be taken out in public frequently, particularly during their early formative months. Take your dog for walks and encourage people to pet and speak to him. This is not usually hard to arrange, since the American Eskimo is so beautiful that he, naturally, attracts attention whereever he goes.

Most Eskies are devoted to children. Here Missy and Kelly Knipe pose with their friend, Gr. Ch. 'PR' Denali's Country U-Kay-C, owned by Nancy Hofman.

As with all dogs in the Spitz family, the American Eskimo has a tendency to bark. Indeed, some dogs seem to enjoy the sound of their own voices. While this may not be a problem for the country living Eskie, it's apt to be seen as a nuisance in city and suburban situations. Barking is a natural extension of the Eskies' watchdog proclivities. When anything seems amiss, he will announce it, to his owners, with a sharp bark. With his keen sense of hearing, he rarely misses a thing. Young puppies should be reprimanded, with a firm "No," for excessive barking. Soon your dog will learn to separate the real concerns from the imaginary.

Above all, the American Eskimo demands to be a part of your family. For hundreds of years, he has lived in close proximity to his owners. He revels in their love and can become destructive, when denied their attention. The Eskie is not happy being relegated to a kennel run in the backyard. His glorious personality and innate intelligence develop fully, only when he is able to share his master's hearth. He accepts his place, as a member of the family, as his due. With his quick intelligence, he adapts readily to the lifestyle of the family. While an Eskie loves all members of the family, it's not unusual for him to single out one person as his very favorite. He can often be seen following that person about the house. He will lie quietly, while they are busy, but feels that it's his duty to be near them, as their private guardian. I often suspect that he also wants to be close by, in case you have a free moment for a little hugging and affection.

One should never underestimate the intelligence of an American Eskimo. They are "people dogs" and you will find yourself dealing with the dog as though he were another human. It's uncanny how the Eskie has the ability to understand not only your tone of voice, but what you say. You will marvel at how expressive your Eskie can be. His warm eyes and body language, once you come to know him, will tell you volumes. Be forewarned, however, if you let your American Eskimo get the upper hand, you're doomed. He can and will take over your house, if you let him. He will demand to be hugged, when it pleases him...and it always pleases him! While you want to express your affection, you must be careful. Eskies can become spoiled very quickly. Always eager to please, your Eskie lives for your approval. He can look

It's hard to resist an American Eskimo puppy.

extremely dejected and crushed when you discipline him. The American Eskimo hates incurring the wrath of his owner. And yet, discipline him you must. As hard as it may be for him to accept, your Eskie must realize that you're the boss. You will love him and praise him when he acts correctly, but you won't reward poor behavior. The Eskie can be quite headstrong, and you must begin, as early as possible, to curb such behavior.

Many American Eskimos share their homes with other pets. Don't be surprised, however, if your Eskie insists on being number one. Initially, he may resent the presence of another animal. You must, therefore, make certain that you give all your pets an equal amount of affection. Let your

As Sabrina shows, American Eskies are charming and entertaining companions.

Eskie know, in no uncertain terms, that you will not tolerate spats with other animals.

American Eskimos are fun dogs to own. Their keen intelligence, and extraordinary desire to please, make them adept at learning tricks of all kinds. For years, Eskies were the star performers in both circus and rodeo acts. Today, the breed is more apt to demonstrate its prowess and trainability in obedience trials. Spend some time with your Eskie. Play with him and, by all means, train him. Even if you do not wish to obedience train your dog, teach him a few tricks. Eskies delight in learning and are proud of their accomplishments. Whether it's playing ball, catching a frisbee or demonstrating a special trick, Eskies are born hams. There's nothing they love better than showing off. American Eskimos are amazingly agile and quick. Their ability to jump, with little effort, must be seen to be believed.

Don't hesitate to include your Eskie in family outings. He will love to go hiking or camping with you and the family. Take your Eskie along when you go for a swim. While not all dogs will take to the water, many Eskies love it. Mine love the water and even enjoy playing in the rain. No matter what you want to do, the Eskie is up to the challenge.

I must warn potential American Eskimo owners of one complication. *Eskies are habit forming!* It's difficult to stop with just one. You'll soon want another of these beautiful white dogs sharing your home and your heart.

3

Official U.K.C. Standard

GENERAL APPEARANCE: The American Eskimo is a well-balanced, typical model of a northern working type dog. The body is proportioned and balanced. Back length from point of shoulder to root of tail should equal the height from pad to top of withers. The face is Nordic type with triangular ears which are slightly rounded at tips and readily distinguished black points (nose, lips, and eye rims). Has an alert, smooth carriage. The coat should be thick especially around the neck, forepart of shoulders and chest forming a lion-like mane. The rump and hind legs down to the hock are also thickly coated forming the characteristic trousers. The ruff (mane) and long outer guard hairs are more prominent on males than females. The richly plumed tail is carried over the back. They should present a picture of beauty, alertness, strength and agility.

HEAD: One denoting power, being wedge-shaped with broad, slightly crowned skull. Head size should be in proportion to body. The stop should not be abrupt but well defined.

MUZZLE: In proportion to head, medium in length, and covered with short, smooth hairs.

EARS: Should conform to head size, slightly rounded at tips, triangular, held erect, set well apart and covered inside with hair. Ears should softly blend with the wedge-shaped head. Outer part of ears to be covered with short, smooth hairs, longer tufts of hair in front of ear openings. Color inside of ear should be pink or slight tinge of grey.

EYES: Should be slightly oval and not slanted. Should be black to brown set well apart with intelligent expression. Eye rims black for preference but dark brown is permissable. Eyelashes should be white.

NOSE: Leather black to dark brown.

LIPS: Black to dark brown. Saggy flews are objectionable.

TEETH & JAW: Strong jaw with close fitting teeth meeting in a level to

25

scissors bite. A full compliment of sound teeth is preferred.

NECK: Medium length and in proportion to body, strong, carried proudly and erect, blending into shoulders with a graceful arch.

BODY: Strong and compactly built but not too short coupled. Back length from point of shoulder to root of tail should equal the height from pad to top of withers. In the male, both testicles must be in the scrotum.

CHEST & RIBS: Should be strong, show broadness and depth. Depth of chest should be at approximate point of elbows. Ribs should be well-sprung and begin upsweep behind the ninth rib to insure adequate room for heart and lung action. Heart and lung room are secured more by body depth than width. Belly should be slightly tucked up immediately behind the ribs.

BACK & LOINS: Should be straight, level, broad and muscular. Loins should be well muscled and not so short as to interfere with easy rhythmic movement and powerful drive of back legs. Females may be slightly longer in back.

FOREQUARTERS: Front legs should be parallel and straight to the pasterns, elbows close to the body and turned neither in nor out. Pastern should be strong and flexible to add spring to movement. Length of leg should be proportioned to body size for a total even balance. Should show have a 45 degree lay back and be firmly set. Front legs well feathered on back side. Dewclaws may be removed at the owner's option.

HINDQUARTERS: Upper thighs should be well developed and muscled. Stifles approximately 30 degree lay off pelvis, hocks well let down and sharply defined. Hind legs should be parallel when viewed from the rear in a natural stance, they should turn neither in nor out. Dewclaws are objectionable on hind legs and should be removed for dogs own safety. The hind legs should be muscular and of adequate bone to blend with body size, the dog should not appear clumsy or racy.

FEET: Should be oval in shape, compact, well padded with hair, pads should be tough and deeply cushioned. Feet should neither "toe in" nor "out" in a normal stance.

TAIL: Should be set moderately high just below top line, covered with long, profuse hair and carried over the back, not necessarily centered, when alert and moving. Sometimes dropped when at rest. Tail bone should come to hock when down. Tightly curled or double hook is a fault.

COAT: The body should be covered with soft, thick, short undercoat, with a longer, guard hair growing through it forming the outercoat, and should be free from any curl, and wave. There should be a noticeably thicker mane covering the neck area, forming the ruff. Length of the outer coat will differ from dog to dog. Quality is more important that quantity.

COLOR: Most desirable is pure white. Permissible are white with biscuit cream, or cream.

MOVEMENT: The American Eskimo should trot, not pace. They should have a quick agile stride that is well timed. The gait should be free, balanced and vigorous, with good reach in forequarters and good driving power in the hind-quarters; when trotting there should be a strong rear action drive. Moving at a walk or slow trot they will not single track, or brush, but as speed increases the legs gradually angle inward until the pads are falling on a line directly under the longitudinal center of the body. The back should remain strong, firm and level.

DISPOSITION: Intelligent, alert and energetic, loyal, friendly but conservative; overly aggressive and overly shy dogs should be penalized.

SIZE: Miniature: Males 12" up to and including 15". Females 11" up to and including 14". Puppy class **only** minimum height could be male 11" and female 10".
   Standard: Males over 15" and up to and including 19". Females over 14" and up to and including 18".

FAULTS: Flop ears, pink or white eye rims, pink nose, pink lips, overshot or undershot bite, roachback, camel back, razor back, straight stifles, cowhocks, splay feet, double curl in tail, tightly curled tail, curly coat, stilted gait, crabbing, crossing over in front, hackney action.

DISQUALIFICATIONS: Any color other than white, biscuit or cream. Blue eyes. Any alterations of dog. Viciousness. Dogs that are cryptorchid or monorchid, deaf or blind.

SCALE OF POINTS

General appearance...15
Movement...15
Head...10
Coat...10
Chest and Ribs...10
Forequarters...10
Hindquarters...10
Back...10
Feet/Legs...5
Tail...5
Total Points...100

A vision of beauty—an American Eskimo puppy. This little charmer is owned by Charline Dunnigan, Cascade American Eskimos. (Carl Lindemaier photo)

4

Selecting an American Eskimo

Buying your first American Eskimo is exciting. You've probably met an Eskie owned by someone else and can't wait to have one of your own. It's better to slow down, however, and give some hard thought to your purchase. After all, the American Eskimo is a long lived breed and this dog will be with you for many years. It's best not to dash out and buy the first cute puppy you see. The more that you learn about the breed, the better your chance of finding a dog that will suit your needs and provide you with years of companionship and joy.

WHAT DO YOU WANT?

What part will the dog play in your life? Are you looking for a pet that will be a wonderful companion? Many Eskies come to be regarded as "one of the family." Do you have children in your home? Perhaps you are buying an American Eskimo that will serve primarily as your children's companion. Have you always dreamed of having a show dog? Dog showing is a wonderful hobby and, of course, it's more fun to win than lose. Will you want to breed your dog? If so, quality will be a consideration. You won't want to buy a dog with a serious fault if you plan on eventually showing or breeding. Do you want a standard sized American Eskimo or would a miniature be more to your liking? All of these things will have to be taken into consideration.

A responsible breeder can be a great help to you in locating just the right dog. In order for him to do this, however, you'll have to be honest with him. Tell the breeder what you want. Remember, the breeder has invested time, effort and money in his dogs. His concern for them extends far beyond the money he will receive. No breeder wants to hear complaints and no buyer wants to be disappointed with his purchase. With cooperation, both of you can be satisfied. You'll have the dog that suits you and fulfills your needs, and the breeder will know that his dog has found a loving home.

WHERE TO BUY

Where can you locate a breeder of American Eskimos? There are a variety of ways to find a breeder. By perusing your local newspaper, you may be able to locate a nearby breeder. You can also contact the United Kennel Club (100 E. Kilgore Rd., Kalamazoo, MI 49001-5598). They will be glad to provide you with a list of American Eskimo clubs and breeders.

If you're looking for a dog for breeding or show, you should definitely subscribe to the UKC's publication, *Bloodlines*. You'll find information on shows, articles concerning Eskies and, of course, advertisements from serious breeders. If there's a show in your area, by all means, plan to attend. You will have the opportunity to see dogs from a variety of kennels and will be able to determine what you like. Other dog magazines may be helpful, too. They sometimes contain advertisements for American Eskimos. The bulk of Eskie advertising, however, is carried in *Bloodlines*.

American Eskimos are occasionally seen in pet shops. Generally, it's best to steer clear of pet shop puppies. Since most reputable breeders refuse to sell puppies to pet shops, you're likely to pay a high price for a poor quality pup. In addition, the pet shop will be able to provide you with only sketchy information on the breed. You're far better off dealing with a breeder who knows the Eskie and is committed to the breed. If a problem should arise, the breeder will be there to assist you.

If you are fortunate enough to locate a breeder in your area, definitely make an appointment to visit his home or kennel. Do your own overall evaluation. Is the kennel clean? Do the dogs look well cared for? Be aware that most Eskie bitches lose their coat and look unkempt when they produce a litter. You may want to ask the breeder for a photo which shows the bitch in proper coat. If you plan to breed your Eskie, ask the owner if he exhibits his stock in shows. Watch the breeder and see how he relates to his dogs. Look for a breeder who is knowledgeable, takes pride in his dogs, and obviously loves them.

If you cannot locate a breeder within driving distance, don't despair. Many breeders are willing to ship a dog to you. Since you won't be able to meet the breeder in person, nor see his dogs, don't hesitate to ask questions. Request photos of the dog. Even via long distance, the breeder will be glad to help you.

ESKIES AND CHILDREN

Dogs and children have a unique rapport. In fact, owning a pet can be a very special experience for a child. A dog can provide a youngster with unconditional love and a deep sense of friendship. Psychologists have recently discovered that dogs and children develop especially close bonds. By using dogs, they have managed to reach many emotionally disturbed and withdrawn children. Dogs also aid in developing the growing child's character. By caring for and training the dog, children learn responsibility. The dog/child bond also helps to instill a sense of understanding, kindness and compassion.

If the dog is to serve as your child's pet, there are some factors that must be borne in mind. No matter how desperately the child wants an American Eskimo, parents must remember that dog ownership is a family venture. As a parent, you have ultimate responsibility for the dog. You must teach the child how to care for and handle the dog properly. If the child forgets to feed the dog,

Eskies are happiest when they can be close to their owners, as Gr. Ch. "PR'
Sassi's Crystal Misty and Leroy Bean illustrate.

then you must willingly step in. You must be prepared to care for the dog
without resentment. If you don't want the dog every bit as much as your child
does, then don't make the purchase.

PURCHASING A PET

While most breeders hope to have a whole litter of show quality puppies,
this rarely happens. It's far more likely that there will be pups in each litter who
lack some fine point required for success in the show ring. Such "pet quality"
puppies are usually available at a lower price. This can be a boon for the person
seeking a companion. While the puppy may not have what it takes to be a show
winner, he still comes from the same stock as his more illustrious brethren. He's
been reared in the same way and received an identical amount of love and care.

Just because your puppy is labelled as pet quality and costs less, this does
not mean that he's inferior. Indeed, the difference between a show and pet
quality puppy may not be outwardly discernible. A puppy with a slight
underbite may appear to be equal or superior to his champion brother. This
fault, however, will prohibit him from winning in the ring, and so he is sold as
a pet and should not be bred. This does not in any way impair the dog's ability
to function as a wonderful companion. The pet quality dog is every bit as
intelligent and loving as his show quality littermates.

In purchasing a pet, temperament will be of prime importance. By
closely observing a litter, you'll see indications of future temperament. Spend
some time watching the litter at play. See how they interact with people,
including their breeder. Chances are you'll be able to spot the most aggressive
pup, the quiet one and the one who's most attentive. You want a sensible puppy

31

with a stable personality. You should be aware that American Eskimos are somewhat aloof and do not always go willingly to strangers. Give the puppies time to relax and come to you. Avoid the puppy that is overly shy or who struggles and growls when you pick him up. Pet owners often say that their puppy "chose them." That's not a bad way to go.

SHOW AND BREEDING STOCK

A show quality puppy is one who conforms to the standard and can be expected to win in the show ring. It can be tricky to pick future show winners. The only guaranteed way to be assured of getting a show quality dog is to purchase an older dog who's already out there consistently winning. Still, if you have your heart set on a puppy, there are some points to bear in mind. Familiarize yourself with the standard, learn what you like and choose a breeder whose stock appeals to you. A breeder who's been working with his bloodline for years, and knows how his stock matures, will have a good idea which puppies will grow into superior Eskies. He will have the advantage of knowing how the puppy's ancestors matured and what they looked like at a young age.

Expect to pay more for the show quality puppy. You may also find that the show quality pup is slightly older. The breeder may well have recognized his potential and held him until a show home could be found. Since the breeder has more invested in the puppy, he'll ask a higher price.

In choosing the show quality puppy, there are certain things you'll want to see. It's obvious that the dog should not have any points listed as faults in the standard. A good head, sound legs, a strong topline, a properly carried tail and good movement are musts. Be sure that the puppy's eyes are dark brown or black. Look closely at his pigmentation. The eyerims, lips and nose should be black. If these areas are partially pink, speckled with black, the dog will probably mature with proper pigmentation. Avoid the dog whose pigmentation appears white. When he's full grown, he probably won't have the black points that are so desirable in the breed. Some puppies will have their ears entirely up at eight weeks. Others will have their ears partially erect. If the pup's ears aren't completely up, look for strong ear leather. Take a look at the coat. Some puppies will have a cream colored cast on their heads. This usually disappears as the puppy

A natural team—Eskies and kids. Here Steven Stevens, Jr. poses with Ch. 'PR' Stevens Snow Queen and Lucky's D-C Ember.

32

grows. The coat should appear thick and lustrous. In addition, look for that "something extra." A dog which exudes that indefinable "class" will generally go far. If you are looking at a group of show quality puppies and there's one you just can't take your eyes off, pick him.

There are additional points you should keep in mind. You want your American Eskimo to be capable of producing healthy, strong puppies of good quality. Look for the dog who comes from a long line of healthy dogs. Females should descend from a line

Children who grow up with dogs often learn about love, compassion and responsibility.

of bitches who whelp easily and freely. Finally, look for the names of males and females, in the pedigree, who have a reputation for producing top quality offspring. If your Eskie comes from a long line of males and females who've produced champions, he's most likely to continue the tradition.

PAPERS AND REGISTRATION

Make sure you receive the United Kennel Club registration papers when you buy your dog. In the 1930's, the U.K.C. registered the "PR," or "Purple Ribbon" designation, with the United States Department of Commerce. Dogs with six generations of purebred ancestors, with three generations registered with the U.K.C., earn "PR" status. All Eskies now carry the "PR" designation.

The back of the green Registration Certificate, or "Bill of Sale," should be filled out at the time of purchase. The seller will fill in the date, his city, state, zip code and signature. You should fill in your name, address, phone number and signature. If you wish to change the dog's name, do it now. While the dog's name can be changed, his registration number always remains the same. Don't be surprised if the breeder insists that you include his kennel name as part of the dog's official registered name. If you're dealing with an out of town breeder, who will be shipping the dog to you, he will probably fill in the Bill of Sale for you. Be sure to sign your name and send the form to the U.K.C. You will receive your permanent purple registration papers, complete with a pedigree, in four to six weeks. A knowledgeable breeder will gladly answer your questions about U.K.C. procedures. For any other questions, contact the U.K.C.

Be leery of buying a puppy if the breeder does not have the registration papers. If the papers have not yet arrived, and you really want the puppy, take a few precautions. Make up your own Bill of Sale giving the puppy's birthdate and stating that he is eligible for registration. Ask for the names, registration numbers and birth dates of both the sire and dam. Both you and the breeder should sign this paper. If you have this information, and don't get your papers, you will be able to turn to the U.K.C. for assistance. They will judge your situation, on a case-by-case basis, and may be able to help you register the pup.

SELECTING A HEALTHY PUPPY

Of course, you want to select a healthy puppy. Even though you aren't a veterinarian, there are some indicators you can check. Look for an overall healthy appearance. The pup's eyes should be clear and bright, not runny. His coat should look healthy and free of any rough patches or bald spots. Lift up the lip and look at the gums. They should be bright pink. Avoid a pup with white gums, as he may have a severe case of worms. Look at his ears and make sure that they are clean, with no waxy buildup. If the pup continally shakes his head, he might have a case of ear mites. Avoid puppies that sneeze or cough. Watch the puppies play and see if they appear frisky and alert. These are good overall indicators of health.

Ask the breeder to write out the dates when your puppy received its shots. If he gave the shots himself, ask for the type of vaccine used. He should also tell you when the next shots are due. Most reputable breeders will allow you to take the puppy to a veterinarian for an exam. Ask how long you have to take the puppy to the vet. Most breeders will allow 24 hours. If it's a weekend, extra time should be granted. Make certain that the breeder will return your money or allow you to select another pup, if the dog fails the exam.

Two beauties! Julie Grizzel Meyers poses with future Gr. Ch. 'PR' Sierra's Panda Bear, owned by Charline Dunnigan. (Stefani photo)

Ask the breeder how often the dog is fed and what feed he's been using. Even if you intend to change the dog's feed, it's best to keep him on the diet he's accustomed to for the first few days. You can then introduce the new food gradually, by mixing it with his current diet. This will help to eliminate digestive upsets. It's also a good idea to find out when the dog had his last meal. Stop by the grocery or pet store and pick up the food recommended by the breeder. Ask the breeder for enough food for the next feeding. If you are purchasing the dog on a weekend and fear that you won't be able to locate the appropriate food, offer to pay the breeder for several days supply.

Now that you finally have your American Eskimo puppy, take him home and enjoy him. He'll soon worm his way into your heart and you won't be able to imagine how you got along without him. You'll quickly discover why owners become sold on this breed.

34

5

Caring for Your American Eskimo

American Eskimos are beautiful, devoted and endearing companions. Most people who have owned an Eskie (or been owned by one), will consider no other breed. We are indeed fortunate that our breed is blessed with good health. While problems can occur in individual dogs, of course, there are no widespread health or genetic problems associated with the Eskie. Since these dogs become important family members, we are also fortunate that they are long lived. It's not unusual for Eskies to reach the age of 12-15 years. To insure that your American Eskimo lives a happy, healthy, full life, you, his owner, need to care for him sensibly. With proper care, you'll be able to enjoy the companionship of your Eskie for many, many years.

SETTING THE RIGHT TONE

If your American Eskimo is to become a pleasurable companion, it's necessary to establish the right tone in your relationship from the very beginning. Eskies, particularly young puppies, are adorable. Beneath that cute exterior, however, can lie the heart of a tyrant. Even the smallest puppy can be amazingly willful. New dog owners are often apt to give in to their demanding youngster. You may think it's amusing to watch your Eskie puppy growl and attack someone's pants leg. When he's full grown and the person he attacks is a small child or your frail, elderly grandmother, it's going to seem less charming. From the very beginning, strive for a well mannered and well trained dog. It's possible to be kind, generous and loving with your dog, without being indulgent and spoiling him unnecessarily.

To achieve this, it's best to decide that you will discipline your pup from the day you get him. Your Eskie must know that you love him and you will be kind to him. However, he should also know that you are the boss and when you give an order it is not to be ignored. You'll be perfectly happy to lavish him with affection, but only when he pleases you and acts correctly. You will not tolerate a dog that's "spoiled rotten." Be patient, be firm and be consistent. Your dog will come to understand what's expected of him.

PROTECTING YOUR ESKIE

While your Eskie is a rugged dog, you must safeguard him. This is particularly important when he's a puppy. Adult dogs will have learned what you consider on and off limits, but puppies are intensely curious and you will have to look out for them.

Puppies are wiggly and unpredictable. You need to understand this and exercise caution. You must take care that your puppy doesn't fall. Young puppies can leap from your arms in the wink of an eye, and a spill may result in injury. Be sure to hold your Eskie close to your body with a firm grip. If he's sitting on your lap, keep a cautionary hand on him. Puppies will learn to evaluate heights as they mature. Don't place your Eskie puppy on a couch or chair until he's large enough to jump there himself. It should go without saying that it is never correct to pick up an Eskie puppy, or adult, by the scruff of his neck or by his front legs. Instead, place one hand between his front legs and, supporting his rear legs with your other hand, lift him smoothly and gently.

If your home has slippery floors, do not permit your Eskie to play vigorously on this surface. This is particularly important when you have a young puppy. He could dislocate his hips, stifles or shoulders at this tender age.

If you have stairs in your home, keep your puppy off them. As your Eskie matures, you can allow him access to the stairs. It's best, however, to train him

With lots of love and proper care, the American Eskimo is a superb companion. This is National Gr. Ch. 'PR' Shelton's Alexander, owned by Jennifer Walker.

to use them safely. Place the dog on the top step and urge him down two or three steps. Take it slow. Within a few days, he'll be capable of managing the stairs.

Swimming pools can also pose a serious hazard to young puppies. Young puppies should be kept far away from swimming pools, unless they have a secure covering. Be sure to check the cover, periodically, to insure a tight fit. When your puppy gets older, you can teach him to swim. Before uncovering the pool, make sure your dog has the ability to swim its length. You must also make certain that your dog knows where the steps are located, so that he can get out when he's through swimming.

Puppies are, by nature, inquisitive. Just as you would with a human baby, you'll have to teach your puppy not to put everything into his mouth. Try to make a tour of your home, searching the floor. That straight pin or rubber band could cause considerable damage to your puppy's stomach. Make certain your Eskie does not have access to any cleaning agents. Decorative figurines or breakable ashtrays should be placed out of reach, too. It's best to remove houseplants from the puppy's vicinity, too. Many houseplants are poisonous. Be certain your puppy doesn't chew on telephone cords or electric wires. Be patient, be firm. While the puppy may drive you to distraction, he'll soon learn what's expected of him.

WHERE WILL YOUR ESKIE SLEEP?

The grown Eskie will generally select his own spot for sleeping. It may be a favorite chair, a warm spot by the fireplace or he may want to share your bed. For the puppy, however, you should provide a bed of some kind. This is best until your Eskie is fully housebroken and can be trusted. There are a variety of dog beds on the market and they range from the simple to the elaborate. However, it's best to avoid wooden or wicker beds. Puppies have a tendency to chew on these materials, while teething. Metal beds, with foam rubber mattresses, covered in a washable fabric are quite practical.

You may want to purchase a dog crate, such as the ones used by the airlines for shipping dogs. This will allow your dog to have his own private place, where he can feel secure and safe. The crate will come in handy if you plan on taking your dog to shows, or traveling with you. Miniature Eskies will be most comfortable in a number two sized crate, while a number three sized crate is ideal for Standard sized Eskies. To insure proper ventilation, you may wish to drill additional air holes in the crate.

FEEDING YOUR ESKIE

Dog owners today are truly blessed to have, at their fingertips, an amazing array of scientifically balanced dog foods. You may choose to feed your American Eskimo a dry dog meal, a canned food or a semi-moist feed. Most breeders recommend a dry kibble. No matter which kind of food you select, you should examine the label to make sure that it's "nutritionally

complete." This will insure that your dog gets the proper blend of protein, fats, vitamins and minerals.

American Eskimos thrive on a variety of diets. Over the years, most breeders have experimented and determined the diet that best suits their dogs. Ideas about the proper diet for an Eskie vary. This simply illustrates that there is more than one way to feed an American Eskimo and still maintain his condition. Unlike people, most dogs thrive on monotony. They are creatures of habit. Once you find a food that is palatable to your dog, it's best to stick with that food, rather than continuously switching brands. Encourage your dog to develop good feeding habits. Ideally, he should consume all his food

A delightful combination—Eskies and children! Neecole Murdesich has learned to care for her puppy. (Doug Kaz photo)

within minutes of your setting it out for him.

Breeders are often asked how many times a day an American Eskimo should be fed. Growing puppies need twice as many calories as an adult dog. Depending on the puppy's age, he may require two to four feedings a day. It's best to check with the breeder, or your veterinarian, and follow their recommendations. Adult dogs need only one or two meals per day. Most dogs appreciate regularity. It's best to feed them at approximately the same time every day. This is one of the best ways to instill good eating habits.

The American Eskimo owner should guard against handing out tidbits to his dog. It's awfully hard to convince your Eskie that he's not entitled to share in your midnight refrigerator raid. If you're munching on something, while watching television, your dog will, undoubtedly, try to convince you that he wants a snack, too. Instead, purchase dog biscuits and parcel out a couple per day. They'll help to keep your dog's teeth clean and won't add empty calories. You can, of course, provide your dog with bones. Just remmeber, poultry and chop bones can be dangerous. Poultry bones, particularly, are likely to splinter and lodge in your dog's digestive tract.

Be sure to provide your dog with plenty of fresh, clean water. Ideally, he should have water available to him whenever he's awake. However, it's best to avoid allowing your dog to drink too much cold water after a hard play period. Give him a small drink, and when he's quieted down, offer more.

HOUSEBREAKING YOUR ESKIE

Most owners prefer to train their dogs, from an early age, to eliminate outside in the yard. Apartment owners, however, sometimes prefer to have their dogs paper trained. For others, paper training may be an interim measure. If a puppy was purchased during winter, and the harsh weather makes it unsuitable to take him outside, paper training may be employed until the weather improves. Whichever method you use, you'll want to begin housebreaking as soon as you bring your new dog home.

One of the important factors in housebreaking a puppy is vigilance. You want to catch the puppy before he has an accident. If you note your dog beginning to squat, say "No" in a harsh voice. This will usually stop him momentarily. It will enable you to pick him up and place him on the paper or carry him to the yard. If the puppy has an accident and you're right there, scold him. Take him immediately to his paper or the yard so that he learns to understand that this is what you want. If you discover that he's had a previous accident, just quietly clean it up. It will do no good to castigate him for an accident made an hour before. Hitting the dog with a rolled up newspaper is, likewise, not necessary or very effective. When the dog does his duty, either on the papers or in the yard, praise him profusely. You may feel stupid praising a dog for going to the bathroom, but it is beneficial. Your compliments of "good dog" will get the message across.

While housebreaking your dog, it's best to restrict his range within the house. Confine him to the kitchen, for instance, if you can't supervise his movements. If he is loose in the house, make certain to keep an eye on him at all times. That way, you'll be able to intervene if he starts

A beautifully cared for Eskie. This is Ch. 'PR' Maxwell's Amiego, owned by Tom & Ruth Maxwell.

to have an accident. Watch your dog closely and learn his habits. Many dogs will sniff the floor or turn in circles before they begin to eliminate. This can serve as a good warning for you. Tell the dog, "No," scoop him up and carry him outdoors or to his paper.

There will be certain times when your dog is most likely to relieve himself. You should take him out first thing in the morning and last thing at night. You'll also want to take him outside or to the paper after each meal or after he's been drinking water. Dogs are often most prone to relieve themselves after a play period. By taking your dog out at these critical times, you'll avoid most accidents.

If you are paper training your Eskie, begin by spreading newspapers over a large area of the floor. Try to determine precisely where you want the papers to lie. You don't want to continually move them and confuse the dog. If, for some reason, you find it necessary to shift the papers to a different location, do this gradually. Day by day, slide the papers closer to the desired spot. All papers containing bowel movements, should be removed as soon as possible. It's often beneficial, however, to leave a paper spotted with urine. This will entice the dog to return to the spot. Gradually, as your dog consistently uses the papers, you can remove some of them. You'll no longer need to cover such a wide area.

Housebreaking a dog can, at times, be frustrating. However, American Eskimos are naturally clean dogs. Most will learn what's expected of them in short order. Some will be housebroken in a matter of days. Occasionally, one will encounter a dog who takes weeks to become trustworthy. Don't despair or become discouraged. Screaming and yelling will only make the whole situation more tense. Just follow the rules outlined above and stick by them.

Providing chew toys can help the puppy and your possessions make it safely through the teething period.

The result of proper care and training. This is Gr. Ch. 'PR' Winterset's Windwalker, owned by Lila & Leroy Bean.

LEASH BREAKING

Most American Eskimos are easy to leash break. Occasionally, however, one can get a stubborn dog who objects to having anything around his neck. This type of dog can be trained. It will just take a little longer and require more patience. Your dog may be fully lead broken after only one session. A headstrong dog may require a week or more of work.

It's advisable to introduce your Eskie to the leash gradually. A light-weight, one piece show lead is best for leash breaking, but you may also use a nylon slip (choke) collar and regular leash. Place the leash or collar around your dog's neck. Call his name and talk excitedly to him. Try walking him back and forth. Talk to him all the while, telling him how good he is. You may want to snap your fingers or make little clicking noises. You'll soon learn what is best for keeping your dog's attention. Remember, you must make this fun. If your dog follows you, praise him enthusiastically. Repeat this for a few minutes each day for the next week.

If your dog objects to walking on the leash, you'll have to take the training a little more slowly. Sit down on the floor with your dog. Place the leash on him and spend a few minutes playing with him. Try letting him run around with the leash on. Be sure to keep a close eye on him. You don't want him to get wrapped around the leg of a chair or caught on something. Pick up the end of the lead. Follow the puppy around, holding the lead, while he explores. Stop and encourage the dog to come to you. If he refuses, kneel down and tap your fingers on the floor. This will usually attract his attention and get him to come. Should he still refuse, very gently pull him to you. Once he gets to you, pick him

41

up, cuddle him and tell him how wonderful he is for responding. Now, try walking again. If your dog should balk, you'll have to begin all over again. You might try turning and walking away from the dog. Most dogs will quickly follow you. Some headstrong dogs will firmly plant their feet and refuse to move. One occasionally encounters a dog who leaps about like a bucking bronco. He spins in the air and won't keep all four feet on the ground. For this type of dog, persistence is the answer. Just keep giving him short sessions where you make it clear that you expect him to walk. Sooner or later, he will realize that you aren't going to give up.

YOUR ESKIE'S HEALTH

Your Eskie will need periodic veterinary visits to safeguard his health. Routine vaccinations will help to protect him. All dogs should be vaccinated, on a yearly basis, for distemper, hepatitis, leptospirosis and parvovirus. You may also wish to have your dog immunized to prevent kennel cough, or parainfluenza. Check with your veterinarian to determine if there are any diseases prevalent in your region and if a vaccine is available to protect your dog. Thanks to modern vaccines, many highly contagious diseases are almost a thing of the past. Your American Eskimo will also need a rabies vaccination. Check with your vet to determine how often this should be given. Some states require yearly inoculations while others stipulate that vaccination should be given once every three years.

It's a good idea to take your dog to a veterinarian once or twice a year for a general routine examination. Such periodic check-ups will help to detect any problems, before they become serious. Take along a stool sample so your vet can examine it microscopically for worms. If your vet finds evidence of worms, he can supply you with the appropriate medication. Ask your veterinarian if heartworm is prevalent in your area. A simple preventative medication, given daily or monthly, will prevent infestation.

By feeding your Eskie properly, caring for his health and grooming him regularly, you'll insure that he stays in prime condition. Consistent training and discipline will help him to become an ideal companion. Be sure not to forget the most important ingredient of all...LOVE, and lots of it! American Eskimos thrive on love and attention. By building a close rapport with your dog, he'll become your true friend.

6

Grooming Your American Eskimo

The American Eskimo's coat is his glory. A healthy dog, with a well groomed, pristine white coat, is a beautiful sight. For all his great wealth of hair, however, the American Eskimo is surprisingly easy to groom. This is a natural breed, and professional trimming or grooming is not necessary.

It is the composition and texture of the Eskie's coat that makes it so easy to maintain. The undercoat is soft, short and thick, while the outercoat is composed of longer guard hairs. This double coat serves to insulate the Eskie from both heat and cold. The length of your Eskie's coat may vary, somewhat, with your local climate. Dogs kept in harsh winter climates tend to grow thicker, more profuse coats. Interestingly, in summer, the Eskie's coat also provides valuable protection. The white color reflects, rather than absorbs, the rays of the sun. Even in the hottest climates, the coat of the American Eskimo should *never* be shaved.

Your Eskie will feel and look better if he is groomed regularly. During grooming sessions, you will have an opportunity to closely observe your Eskie's condition. Often potential medical problems can be detected, before they become serious. You will be able to see cuts or growths, feel abscesses or lumps beneath the skin, spot broken or ingrown nails, smell strong ear odor and see tartar buildup on the teeth. Burrs or thorns can be removed promptly, before they cause trouble. If, despite the best of care, your American Eskimo's coat looks lackluster, dry or brittle, you should check with your veterinarian. It may be that your dog has an internal condition, such as worms, that is affecting the coat.

PUPPY GROOMING

American Eskimo puppies have a beautiful, fluffy, fast growing coat. It's best to acquaint your new puppy with the grooming routine, soon after you get him. Your little Eskie will quickly adapt to the routine and come to enjoy it. There are a few important rules, however, for grooming pups. First and foremost, be gentle with your pup. By handling him carefully and being patient with him, he will learn to look forward to your grooming sessions.

Never groom your Eskie when you are tense or upset. While this is an important rule for Eskies of any age, it is especially crucial with puppies. Speak to the dog, as you groom him, in a calm tone of voice. Keep those first grooming sessions short. Encourage the dog to stand still as you groom him. And last, but certainly not least, tell your Eskie how good he was, when you are through with the sessions. Remember, Eskies thrive on praise. Telling the pup that he's very good, and looks beautiful, will please him to no end. You may even want to conclude the session with a small tidbit, as a reward. Soon, your dog will look forward to the routine as a special time you spend together.

WHAT WILL I NEED?

A few simple tools are all that's required to groom your American Eskimo. First, and foremost, you will need a good bristle brush that's comfortable to work with. A wide-toothed comb is a must. It's also best to purchase shedding and dematting tools. All of the above can be purchased through dog supply catalogs or at your local pet shop. A hair dryer is a real help. It's not necessary to buy one of the heavy duty types generally recommended for dogs, unless you have many Eskies to care for. A small, yet sturdy, hand held blow dryer will suit your purposes. You will need a good shampoo, preferably with a whitening additive. You will also find that a coat conditioner is helpful. Your grooming box should include cotton balls, a styptic pencil, mineral oil, baking soda and nail clippers.

You will need a convenient work place. It's best if the grooming surface provides non-slip footing for the dog and is at a comfortable height for you. This will save wear and tear on your back and give you better control over your dog. You can purchase a specially designed, folding grooming table, with a rubber mat surface and a grooming arm. The owner with just a few dogs, however, can get along well without this. Some Eskie owners do their grooming on the top of their clothes washer or dryer. If this is your choice, a piece of indoor-outdoor carpeting will give your Eskie better footing. I have used the top of my number three sized kennel or crate with success.

BRUSHING

Regular brushing is the most important part of your grooming routine. Eskies should be brushed at least once a week, and twice a week is preferable. This will require a session of approximately fifteen minutes, if the dog is brushed regularly. A proper brushing will help to stimulate and clean your Eskie's coat.

Thorough brushing is a must. While it's tempting, particularly if you are in a hurry, to skimp on the brushing, don't! You will not achieve the desired results by just glossing over the surface. That marvelous, glowing finish is achieved by consistent and diligent brushing. You must be sure to brush right down to the skin. It's best to brush slowly, gently and methodically, so that you

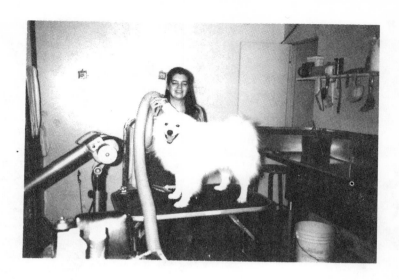

If you introduce your American Eskimo to grooming from the start, he will learn to enjoy the process.

get every hair on the dog. Heavy handed treatment will only serve to remove the undercoat. I generally brush the coat down first and then back-brush the coat up toward the head. This gives the dog a fluffy, downy appearance.

While brushing, pay special attention to the particularly dense areas of the coat. The ruff, or mane, must be thoroughly brushed to prevent matting. After you've brushed the ruff, you may wish to follow up, by combing it with a wide-toothed comb. This will insure that they are no mats and will remove any loose hair. Special attention should also be paid to the hair on on the hind legs, called the trousers, and the tail.

When you've finished brushing your Eskie, use the comb on the hair around the ears and armpits. These areas are prone to matting, and you will often find small knots or snaggles. If left unattended, these can develop into clumps or mats. Be gentle when combing these areas, as the coat is finer in texture.

REMOVING MATS

Hopefully, with regular brushing, your American Eskimo will not develop mats. However, even the best cared for dogs can get briars, thorns or burrs caught in their coats. At such spots, mats are likely to form. When working on mats, you must be patient. Removing mats can be tedious, time consuming work. Talk lovingly to your dog and offer him a tidbit. By all means, keep a firm hand on him, so he doesn't jump off the grooming table.

There are several methods for dealing with knots and mats. Each owner will have to decide what works best for him. Small knots can usually be teased

45

When brushing your Eskie's coat, pay extra attention to those areas that are most readily prone to matting.

out with the fingers. For larger mats, you may want to use talcum powder or olive oil, and slowly work out the mat, with your fingers. A dematting tool, sometimes called a mat splitter, together with your wide toothed comb, can be useful when dealing with stubborn mats. Take your time and pull a few hairs at a time away from the mat. You can also purchase a detangling preparation, from catalogs, supply houses or pet stores. This preparation can be sprayed on, so the area is fully saturated. Allow the saturated area to sit for a few minutes, before trying to remove the mat. For badly matted areas, it's sometimes necessary to make several applications of the detangling formula. Never yank at a matted clump as this is very painful to the dog.

If you still can't work the mat free, you can use scissors. Using blunt nosed scissors or thinning shears, snip as small an area as possible. Be sure to snip along the grain of the hair. Using your comb, begin working on the area. Never cut across the mat or cut it completely off. Your Eskie will end up with a moth eaten appearance.

If burrs or thorns have become tangled in your Eskie's coat, saturate the object and the hair around it with petroleum jelly, baby oil or olive oil. Then, work it free with your fingers and the comb. Nail polish remover can help to remove gum or sap from an Eskie's coat. Do take care, however, and don't allow the remover to touch the dog's sensitive skin.

Make absolutely certain that your dog has been thoroughly brushed before bathing. Knots, tangles and mats *must* be removed before shampooing. If not, they will clump together and become more firmly set and almost impossible to remove.

SHEDDING

A well groomed American Eskimo sheds surprisingly little. Many factors, however, can affect the degree of shedding. Generally, Eskies kept as house dogs shed more than those who spend much of the time outdoors. Stress also affects the degree of shedding. Physical problems, including allergies, can result in coat loss. Having a litter usually causes most females to shed, or "blow," their coats, and some also shed several weeks after they come in season.

Most American Eskimos blow their coats once a year. Males shed only once annually, while females may shed more often. Usually this occurs in summer, but it can often be influenced by the length of daylight in your area. The coat comes out in great handfuls, and your house will be filled with tufts of snowy hair. To eliminate this, it's best to get rid of the dead hair as quickly as possible. Much of the nuisance of shedding can be eliminated, if the owner will comb out the loose hair when he first notices that the dog is beginning to blow coat. Comb your dog frequently during the shedding period, to remove all the dead hair. Bathing, with warm water, will also help to loosen the dead hair. Again, be sure to give your dog a thorough brushing before bathing.

Your Eskie will look many pounds lighter after shedding. Indeed, you will be surprised at how his appearance changes. For several weeks, you may feel like hiding the naked looking dog. Have no fear, the coat will return. Generally, it takes about two to four months for the American Eskimo's coat to return to its full glory.

BATHING YOUR ESKIE

We often say that the American Eskimo has a "self-cleaning" coat. This is because the texture of the coat naturally repels dirt. When regularly brushed, it is possible for many Eskie's to go months without a bath. Most Eskie owners bathe their dogs every two or three months. Show dogs, however, depending on the show schedule, may need more frequent shampooing, to keep them pristine white. Too much bathing is best avoided, as it dries out the skin and strips the coat of its natural oils. These oils are largely responsible for the coat's self-cleaning quality.

Remember, give your American Eskimo a thorough brushing and remove all mats or tangles, before bathing. While Eskie's can be washed outdoors, with a hose, in warm weather, most breeders prefer to bathe the dogs in a tub. Place a rubber mat, or a towel, in the bottom of the tub to insure good footing. Many dogs become frightened, and difficult to control, when their feet begin to slip on the ceramic surface.

If at all possible, purchase a shampoo which contains a whitener. These are readily available through pet supply catalogs or at pet stores. If you are unable to locate such a shampoo, you can purchase laundry bluing at your grocery store. This is added to the final rinse water. You will also want to get one of the many good coat conditioners on the market today. Only by experimentation will you be able to tell which works best on your Eskie's coat.

The American Eskimo is a double coated breed. It's difficult to get water to penetrate through the undercoat, all the way to the skin. Doubtless, this served the Eskie well when he lived in a northern climate, but it can be frustrating when you are trying to bathe him. Using luke warm water, wet your dog thoroughly before applying the shampoo. Be sure not to get water or shampoo into the ears or eyes. Some people like to place a small plug of cotton in the ears, and a drop or two of mineral oil in each eye.

Apply the shampoo to the coat. lathering the entire body. Work the lather in thoroughly, starting at the head and working your way towards the tail. Be sure not to forget the belly, the armpits and the undersides of the thighs. If you wish, you may allow your Eskie to stand in an inch or so of water. This is helpful, especially if his feet or pasterns have become muddy. They will have the chance to soak clean, while you are working on the rest of the coat. Shampoo your Eskie's face last. Lather the suds between your palms and gently wipe over the muzzle.

Now, it's time to rinse the dog. If your Eskie is particularly dirty, don't hesitate to rinse him, reapply the shampoo, and rinse again. Begin rinsing at the ears and neck, working down the back. Be sure to rinse thoroughly, until you see no traces of suds. Add the coat conditioner and give your Eskie a final rinse. If you are using laundry bluing, add three or four drops to the rinse water and shake it before applying it to your dog. Drain any water that remains in the tub. Now, let your Eskie have a good shake, to get rid of excess water. If he doesn't shake, blowing gently in

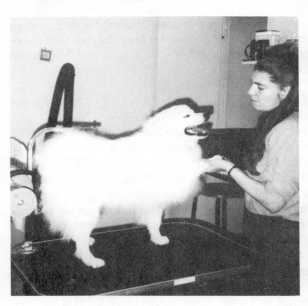

Frequent brushing is the key to a lovely coat that shows off your American Eskimo to its finest appearance.

his ear will usually do the trick.

Take your Eskie out of the tub. Gently towel off the excess water. It's really better to blot the coat dry, rather than rubbing it, which may inadvertently cause tangling. On warm, sunny days, some owners will let their American Eskimos dry naturally, in the sun. You must, however, be absolutely certain that your dog is not exposed to drafts.

Most breeders prefer to blow dry the Eskie's coat. Blow drying should be done while the coat is still damp. Place the blow dryer on the low setting. Aim it at a section of the coat and, with the brush in your other hand, brush up and towards the head. This is usually called backbrushing. Work the coat in sections, using light and easy strokes. The use of the blow dryer is the best way to get that light, airy look that is so extraordinarily beautiful.

That beautiful coat is the result of good grooming. Pictured here is Ch. 'PR' Winterset's Snowfire, owned by Sheila & Frank Ruzanski.

DRY CLEANING

Between baths, it is possible to keep your American Eskimo looking clean and white, with a "dry cleaning." This consists of applying a cleansing agent to the coat, and thoroughly brushing it out. Dry cleaning is excellent when your Eskie has soiled only one spot on his coat. For old dogs, prone to chilling, a thorough dry cleaning can be substituted for a regular bath. This method of grooming is also valuable with puppies and will remove dirt from their coats when a buyer phones unexpectedly and wants to look over the pups.

There are many agents that can be used to dry clean your Eskie. I prefer corn starch, which does an excellent job and is inexpensive. Baby powder and talcum powder can also be used. Of the two, baby powder is preferable. In addition to doing a fine cleaning job, it leaves the dog nice and sweet smelling.

49

Dry clean your Eskie outside, or place a large towel or sheet over your work surface. The dry cleaner should be liberally sprinkled onto the coat. You must make sure that the coat is thoroughly dry, or else you have a sticky mess on your hands. Rub the cleaner in and allow it to remain on the coat for awhile. This gives the cornstarch, or powder, a chance to absorb any dirt or dust in the coat. Now, begin vigorously brushing your Eskie. At first, it will seem as though you are sending smoke signals. Keep brushing until all the powder has been removed. You'll be surprised at how sparkly white your American Eskimo looks.

CLIPPING NAILS

Your American Eskimo needs periodic trimming of his nails. Generally, a once a month clipping is best. Some dogs, particularly those kept on rough surfaces, will wear their nails down naturally. Most dogs, however, will need to have their nails clipped. It's important to keep them clipped back, because nails which are allowed to grow long will cause the feet to splay.

Most breeders use a guillotine type clipper. Some dogs strongly object to having their nails clipped, and you may want an assistant to help you. If your dog puts up a struggle, you might try to shield his eyes, so that he doesn't see the actual clipping. This sometimes helps. Try your best to determine exactly where the quick (vein) in the nail ends. By looking closely at each nail, you will see the pink blood vessel. Place the nail clipper over the nail and cut just before the vein. If you should, accidentally, cut into the vein, just apply a little styptic powder or use a styptic pencil. Each time you cut the dog's nails, the vein will recede slightly. Therefore, the more you clip the dog's nails, the shorter they can be kept.

CLEANING THE EARS

Each time you brush your Eskie, it's best to clean his ears. Fortunately, with their upright ears, American Eskimos rarely have ear problems. The inside of the ear can become dirty, though. I prefer to clean the ears with a cotton ball, moistened with a little mineral oil. Under no circumstances should you probe deeper into the ear than the eye can see.

DENTAL CARE

While you are grooming your Eskie, you'll want to check his teeth. Routine cleaning of the teeth will help to avoid dental problems and prevent the buildup of tartar. I prefer to use a gauze pad and baking soda, for cleaning my Eskies' teeth. It is also possible to use a small toothbrush and human toothpaste. Start with the outside surfaces of the teeth. At first, this may be all your dog will allow you to do. As he gets used to the procedure, you can clean the inside surfaces of the teeth, too.

It's best to accustom your dog to teeth cleaning, from the time he's a pup. Dogs who are not used to the procedure, do not like having their teeth cleaned. It's best to do the cleaning, gently, quickly, yet thoroughly. Be sure to lavish your dog with praise, when you're through. If your American Eskimo has a heavy tartar accumulation, you will have to take more drastic measures. Purchase a metal tooth scraper. These are available through many dog supply catalogs. When scaling the teeth, try not to scrape too vigorously. You want to remove the tartar, but you don't want to chip the coat of enamel covering each tooth.

Be sure to have your veterinarian check your Eskie's teeth once a year. He can spot any trouble areas and recommend treatment. In the meantime, hard bones and dog biscuits will help to prevent the accumulation of tartar.

EYE STAIN

Many American Eskimos experience no problem with eye stain. For others, however, it is a persistent and unsightly problem. Eye staining is a common problem in many coated, white breeds. There are many reasons that eye stain can occur, and pinpointing the root of the problem may lead to an effective treatment. Some dogs are prone to allergies, and excessive tearing of

No wonder the American Eskimo is called "the dog beautiful." The impressive Gr. Ch. 'PR' Sierra's Panda Bear, owned by Charline Dunnigan, is groomed to perfection.

the eyes may be one of the symptoms. Dogs with too round eyes often have a more loosely attached lower eye rim (called the haw). This type of eye is more prone to watering and stain. Eye stain will also result when the tear duct becomes blocked or if hair grows into the eye rim. If your dog is plagued by excessive tearing, it's best to consult your veterinarian. He may be able to detect the problem and prescribe appropriate treatment.

You can try to control the tearing, by applying vaseline to the area beneath the eye. This is sometimes helpful and will help the tears to roll off, rather than sinking in and staining. If your dog stains easily, moisten a cotton ball with warm water and attend to the eyes daily. *Blot* up the tears. *Do not rub* them away. You may want to try shaving off the badly stained hair. This, combined with daily cleaning of the area, may take care of the problem. The new hair will grow in white. However, if you have not discovered the root cause of the problem, the hair will quickly become stained once again. Some breeders have found that a daily application of cornstarch helps to prevent staining.

GROOMING YOUR ESKIE FOR THE SHOW RING

There's nothing more beautiful than a ring full of American Eskimos, groomed to perfection. You will quickly see why this breed has been christened "The Dog Beautiful." The United Kennel Club's rules are very specific, regarding show ring presentation. Absolutely no altering of the coat is permitted. The Eskie is not trimmed and the whiskers are left intact. There is, however, one bit of minor trimming that is allowed. You may tidy up the hair around your Eskie's feet. Some American Eskimos grow unsightly tufts of hair around and under their feet. This can prevent your Eskie from getting good traction and can make it very difficult for the judge to assess his movement. These hairs are also likely to get dirty or muddy, and to pick up grass seeds.

If you plan on showing your American Eskimo, you must devote time to grooming him properly. Cleanliness is most important and thorough brushing is a must. The difference between a meticulously brushed and a superficially brushed dog is certain to show. To get that nice beautiful finish, to the coat, takes diligence.

Shows are an excellent place to learn more about grooming. Individual Eskies will have varying coat textures. Some coat conditioners and products will work better with certain types of coats. Don't hesitate to discuss grooming products and procedures with other Eskie owners. Most are more than willing to take the time to discuss coat preparation, for the show ring, with you.

7

The Stud Dog

Great care should be taken in the selection of a stud dog. Whether you are purchasing a male for your own use or planning to pay a fee for the use of an outside dog, much thought should go into the choice. The male American Eskimo can have a tremendous impact on the breed. While a female will have only one, or at most two litters a year, a male can be bred many, many times. He can pass on his good qualities, as well as his faults, to a great number of offspring. Indeed, a very popular stud, used for many years, can have a far-reaching impact on the breed.

What should you look for in a stud dog? Just because a male is a registered purebred, he is not automatically qualified to be a stud. Even those interested only in breeding pets should still be guided by the standard and attempt to produce typical American Eskimos. A male intended for stud usage should be a good representative of the breed. While he needn't be a champion, he should, nevertheless, excel in the basic breed virtues and have no glaring faults. A male who has blue eyes, unacceptable color, a poor coat, flopped ears or a bad bite should not be used for breeding. A dog who is structurally unsound would also be a poor candidate for stud use. Size should also be a consideration. Standard sized American Eskimos should measure 15"-19" while Miniatures should be 12"-15". Dogs who deviate from these height specifications, generally, should not be bred. It's best to breed Standards to Standards and Miniatures to Miniatures, rather than intermingling the sizes.

You'll want to make sure that the male has both testicles. A cryptorchid male, or one with no testicles, will be sterile. A monorchid male (one with only a single testicle descended), however, may well be fertile. Monorchidism is a disqualification in the breed ring and, since the condition may well be hereditary, you should avoid the stud with only one testicle.

Pedigree is of great importance when you're deciding on a stud. The pedigree should reflect a background of careful breeding. Since the stud dog passes on the qualities transmitted to him by his ancestors, it will help if you can learn as much as possible about the dogs named in the pedigree. Look for a balanced breeding, with good dogs on both sides of the stud's pedigree. It may be tempting to use a dog sired by "Grand Champion 'PR' Mr. Wonderful," but if his mother was "'PR' Little Miss I have Every Fault" then you are just as likely to get puppies resembling the grandmother as you are Mr. Wonderful.

The real "proof of the pudding," with a stud dog, is how well he can produce. The effectiveness of a stud dog should be measured by the quality of his progeny. It's a sad fact of life that some spectacular show winners never sire progeny as good as themselves. Conversely, some less flashy dog may consistently produce outstanding offspring. If you are using an outside stud, try to obtain as much information as possible about the quality of the American Eskimos he has produced. If you are using one of your own studs, keep detailed records and photos of his offspring. Check back with puppy buyers and try to see (in person or in photos) how the puppies matured. This way you will be able to see if your dog is living up to his potential as a stud.

The famous Gr. Ch. 'PR' Hofman's Country Diamond, a Standard male. 'Country' was the first Grand Champion on the Pacific Coast. His greatest contribution to the breed, however, is in the many Champion and Grand Champion children and grandchildren he has produced. Proud owners are Nancy & Darrel Hofman. (Dai photo)

While physical qualities are undeniably important, don't forget to look for a dog that excels in temperament. A dog passes on not only his conformation, but also his mental characteristics. An Eskie who is markedly shy or overly aggressive is not typical and makes an unsuitable stud dog. You must remember that the majority of your puppies will probably enter pet homes, where temperament will be of prime importance.

Last, but certainly not least, you want a dog who is healthy and vigorous. It's best if he comes from a background of long-lived, healthy dogs. You also want a dog who is a reliable breeder. While a dog's reliability as a stud is often molded by his early breeding experiences, the dog that is uniformly healthy and hardy is most likely to consistently have a good sperm count. Bitches bred to such a vigorous dog are more likely to become pregnant and deliver strong puppies.

All breeders hope that they will have a prepotent stud. This is a male who is dominant for his virtues and can overcome the faults of most bitches. He can be used with success on a wide variety of bitches. Such studs can quickly make a name for a kennel and contribute much to their success. You are indeed fortunate if you discover that you own such a dog. A truly prepotent male comes along rarely, so take advantage of him if you are lucky enough to own one. Don't hesitate to seek the services of a prepotent stud owned by another breeder.

RAISING THE STUD DOG

Experienced breeders have learned that healthy, hardy dogs are most likely to be active, vigorous studs. A good, well-balanced diet, coupled with plenty of exercise, is important for the stud dog. You want him in top-notch condition. Be sure to check for both internal and external parasites. Worms and fleas will sap his energy, and a male in run down condition may well have a below normal sperm count.

The mental attitude of a stud dog is important. You want a lively, confident dog, who is sure of himself and enthusiastic about breeding. Therefore, he must be handled differently than a pet male. At an early age, your male dog will begin to mount and ride other dogs. Do not be upset if you find him trying to mount other males. He may even latch on to your leg and thrust enthusiastically. While it would be acceptable to chastise a pet male, you'll

Out for a walk in the woods is U-CDX 'PR' Kaz Northern Bandit, owned by Doug & Esperanza Kaz.

55

have to be more inventive with the future stud dog. Repeatedly telling him "No," at an early age, may discourage him. You don't want to convey the impression that breeding is wrong. If he's riding your leg, you might try distracting his attention with a favorite toy, or take him out for a walk.

If at all possible, you'll want to breed your dog, for the first time, while he's still young. Many breeders find eighteen months an ideal age to begin. By this time, the male will be physically and mentally mature, and you will be able to accurately assess his quality. Once a male has sired his first litter, he is referred to as a "proven" stud.

That first breeding is very important. You want everything to go well, as this experience will set the tone for future breedings. Take the time to observe your dog's actions closely. You will see how he responds to females in season and how he approaches the mating process. You will also be training your dog to be the type of stud you want. He will learn to respond to your encouragement. You'll aid him by holding the bitch so that he can breed her successfully and efficiently, and you will both learn to function together as a team. While it will take time and patience to accomplish this, you will find that the time is well spent, as you will end up with the type of reliable and eager stud you can always count on.

It's best if your dog's first breeding is to a proven, easily bred bitch. Working with two inexperienced dogs can try the patience of the most experienced breeder. The maiden bitch is likely to flirt and to sit down when the male tries to mount her. Even worse, she may snap at him as he mounts. While some dogs will ignore this, it could confuse and discourage your inexperienced male, and spoil his enthusiasm for breeding. If you have little experience yourself and you must breed two unproven dogs, then it might be wise to obtain the help of an experienced breeder.

The inexperienced male is more apt to flirt and play with the female. Some of this should be permitted for it will increase his excitement. However, you don't want him to get into the habit of playing excessively. You want him to attend to the business at hand. Verbally encourage him. You don't want to talk so much that you distract him, but you do want to let him know that you approve of what he's doing. No matter how frustrated you become, don't lose your pa-

One of Frank Morlock & Paul Donahoo, Jr's. stud dogs, Ch. 'PR' Morlock's King Snowball.

tience. This could ruin the dog for future breedings. Take your time and don't hurry him. He'll soon have the idea.

Some breeders simply put the male and female in a run and leave them alone for several days hoping that they will breed. This is an inefficient and dangerous way of handling a breeding. They have no idea if or precisely when the female was bred. This makes it difficult to plan for the whelping. If you are controlling the breeding and for some reason the stud will not service the bitch, all is not

The lovely Standard male, Ch. 'PR' Lucky's Ruf-E-N, owned by Bruce & Linda Bargmann.

lost. You may still have time to try another stud with the bitch. Also, accidents do occasionally happen and either the bitch or, more likely, the stud could be injured. By controlling the breeding you will be able to avoid a calamity.

It's best to teach your stud dog that you will hold the bitch for him. Some males, particularly those who've bred on their own for the first time, will have nothing to do with a female if you insist on holding her. This can lead to problems when you try him with a difficult bitch. If you are breeding a small stud to a larger female, you may have to reposition the dogs so they can breed successfully. A male who will not allow you to assist will be annoying. Encourage the stud to mount the bitch while you hold her. Beware of talking too much when he's attempting to actually penetrate her. After he's tied, you may indeed pet him and tell him how pleased you are with the job he's done. This way he will learn to be comfortable with having you touch him during the breeding process.

A good stud can continue to sire puppies into his old age. After the age of eight to ten years, however, you may note that some of the bitches he has bred do not conceive. His fertility may diminish during hot weather, for instance. If you're not ready to permanently retire your still valuable stud, you may wish to arrange for periodic sperm counts to be taken.

Some males will undergo a personality change after they are used for breeding. They may begin to mark their territory, lifting their leg on furniture or houseplants. Watch your male carefully, following breeding, and reprimand him if he exhibits such behavior. Aggression can also be a perplexing problem with males used for breeding. This is seldom a problem for males housed in kennels, where they are routinely separated. In a household situation, where another male resides in the home, this can be devastating. It takes stud dogs of superlative character to coexist peacefully in a home environment. You will

57

The miniature stud dog, Mell-O-Bark's Wee Minute Man, owned by Mrs. Janet E. O'Conner, Mell-O-Bark Kennels.

need to monitor the dog's behavior, following breeding, to ensure that there are no squabbles or fights. Because of this, it's best to think very seriously before allowing your household companion to be used at stud.

HANDLING THE MATING

You may want to allow the dogs to become familiar before the breeding. Some owners place the dogs in adjacent runs so that they can become acquainted with each other. If this is your first breeding, it's advisable to have two people on hand to handle the breeding. Once you gain experience, you may be able to deal with the situation by yourself. It's important to be able to control both the dog and the bitch. If you are uncertain, placing a leash on the bitch will give you added control.

Take a few moments to plan for the breeding, before you bring out both dogs. You'll want to do the breeding in an area where the dogs will be free from distraction. It's best if the stud is familiar with the area, so that he will feel comfortable. I prefer to breed dogs in the early morning or the evening. I find this less taxing than during the heat of the day. Examine your male. If he is heavily coated, you may wish to trim any hair that's near the penis. Similarly, if the bitch is heavily coated, you may want to clip the hair around her vulva. You want a surface where your male will have good footing. This is seldom a problem if you are breeding outdoors. If you'll be breeding the dogs in the house, you may want to spread out a piece of old carpeting. Be aware that there may be a few dribbles and be sure to protect your regular carpet. If your stud is smaller than the bitch, you might try placing the dogs on a sloping surface or have a small rug on hand. This can be folded so that the male can stand on it and elevate his height.

Be sure to prepare for your own comfort, too. Once the male penetrates the female, his penis will swell and the dogs will become "tied" together. A tie may last only a few minutes or it could continue for an hour. Most ties last between 15-25 minutes. Try to make yourself as comfortable as you can. If you find a position where you're able to rest your back against a wall, you may be more comfortable. You don't want to be distracted, either. If you're breeding your dogs in the house, take the telephone off the hook. If you're expecting an important phone call, try to move the telephone within reach.

An outstanding Miniature stud dog. U-CD Gr. Ch. 'PR' Winterset's Silver Fox is one of the country's top Eskies, winning fifty Grand Champions classes to date. He is the sire of many Champions and Grand Champions. Proud owners are Sheila & Frank Ruzanski.

If you wish you may allow the dogs to play and flirt for a few minutes. Kneel down on the ground or floor near the dogs and keep one or both hands on the bitch. Hold her firmly with one hand on her shoulders or neck and the other on her belly. After some initial nuzzling and licking, your male will probably start licking the bitch's vulva. If she's ready to be bred, she'll raise her tail and elevate her vulva. The male will then usually mount her. You'll have to be prepared to control the bitch if she starts to snap or tries to lie down. You'll want to try to line up the bitch and the stud. If he is out of position, very gently push him away and encourage him to try again. You will most likely be able to tell when the male has penetrated by the reaction of the bitch. Just make sure she stands solidly on all four feet until he stops thrusting. Your stud dog will probably slide his front feet off the bitch's back. You may notice that he is anxious to turn. Gently help him bring his hind leg over the bitch's back. Both dogs will then be standing tail to tail. If, while he's turning, your male should cry out in pain, quickly bring him back to the original position. You don't want to take the chance of injuring him.

Just when you think your back will break and your legs have gone permanently to sleep, the dogs will separate. It may take you a few seconds to realize that they are no longer linked. Some breeders like to hold the bitch's hindquarters up in the air for a few seconds to avoid losing any sperm. Others consider this a waste of time.

It's best to separate the dogs. Some terrifically enthusiastic stud dogs will mount the bitch and attempt to breed again. Give the dogs some fresh water and allow them to rest. Most breeders skip a day and then breed once more on the following day.

THE OUTSIDE TIE

An outside tie occurs when the bulb, located at the rear of a dog's penis, swells outside the bitch's vagina. An outside tie is more difficult for the inexperienced breeder to handle. Nevertheless, while less desirable than an inside tie, a properly handled outside tie is often successful. Some males seem more prone to outside ties and, while they are more trouble to breed, they can and do sire puppies.

It's best to hold the penis behind the swollen bulb. Place your other hand on the bitch's belly and press her backwards. You can allow the stud to turn, but it's usually easier to keep the pair linked if he remains mounted. You'll want to hold the bitch and stud together as long as possible. Though the dogs may be restless, try to keep them together for at least five minutes.

THE PUBLIC STUD

As the owner of a public stud, you must realize that you are undertaking a great responsibility. You must insure the safety and well-being of any bitch in your care. A nervous female, in strange surroundings, may be more apt to dart

A lovely head shot of the Standard male, 'PR' Ivan Renwick III, owned by John & Marge Renwick.

out a door or escape under a fence. You could be legally liable if she's lost. You will also have to prepare yourself for some inconvenience. It's quite possible that you will have to endure a bitch who barks and whines all through the night.

Some of these problems can be abated by having the bitch's owner accompany her during the actual breeding. Some bitches are comforted when they're held by their owners. Others, however, never calm down sufficiently when their owners are present. They are more likely to be subdued without their owner around. You may be more comfortable without the presence of the owner, too. While you certainly don't want to be abusive to the bitch, it is sometimes necessary to be quite firm, particularly with maiden bitches. Stud owners sometimes find this difficult to do under the watchful eye of the female's owner.

Before you offer your male at stud, give some thought to what policies you wish to adopt. You should breed only to United Kennel Club registered bitches. Standard stud fees are usually equivalent to the price of a show quality puppy. It stands to reason, of course, that the stud fee for a Grand Champion or Champion will be higher than for an untitled male. Unless specific arrangements have been made, stud fees are paid at the time of breeding.

You will have to decide if you're willing to accept the pick of litter pup in lieu of a stud fee. If you do decide to accept a puppy, be sure to specify when

An impressive Miniature male, Ch. 'PR' Sassi's Tid Bit Too, owned by Lynda Lynch.

you will make your choice. Most breeders opt to pick their puppy between eight and twelve weeks. Do try to be considerate. It's unfair to prohibit the litter owner from selling any puppies because you delay in making your pick.

Bitch owners should be told that they are paying for a service only. The fee is for the male's services, and your time and effort. Simply paying a stud fee does not guarantee a pregnancy or live litter. Most breeders will provide a repeat breeding if the bitch fails to conceive.

You should decide if you wish to offer a "return" service. Many breeders promise one free return breeding if the bitch does not conceive. Most breeders specify that the return service is good only on the bitch's next season. Some stud owners require proof, such as a letter from a veterinarian, that the bitch did not whelp a litter. You may also want to specify that you be notified in a given amount of time if the bitch fails to conceive.

Whatever policies you decide upon, it's best to put them in writing. This will help to eliminate misunderstandings. If you frequently provide stud service, you will want to prepare a standard contract which includes all your policies. If you only rarely provide stud service, it's still best to formalize the agreement. A simple list of any terms and conditions, including a receipt of any monies paid, should be signed by both parties. This precaution with take a little time and thought, but it will help to avoid hard feelings and disputes. Such foresight may well prevent a lawsuit.

8

The Brood Bitch

Much of what we've said about stud dog selection, applies equally to the brood bitch. The beginning breeder will make no more important selection than the purchase of a good brood bitch. The strength of your breeding program will be based on your continuing production of good bitches. While many breeders make a grand splash with a sensational winning dog, the true breeder knows that a line of top-producing bitches is his ticket to success. Excellent brood bitches form the cornerstone of the carefully planned breeding program. If you are using outside studs and a breeding proves unsuccessful, it's relatively easy to change course. If, however, your female is unsuitable as a brood bitch, you must either begin again or be plagued with years of trying to breed up from a mediocre start. The brood bitch is the rock upon which the foundation of your kennel will rest. Selection of the appropriate brood bitch, therefore, is essential.

The brood bitch does not necessarily have to be a champion herself. It is imperative, however, that she be carefully bred and from a line that has a reputation for producing consistent quality. After reviewing the breed standard carefully, decide which qualities are most important to you. Select a bitch from a line which excels in those virtues. Look for a bitch who is structurally sound and one that excels in temperament. You'll be on your way to producing American Eskimos of which you can be proud.

BREEDING AGE

American Eskimo females generally come in season for the first time between six and nine months of age. All Ekies are individuals, however, and occasionally you will find bitches who come into season earlier or later than this average. I've heard of Eskies who came into season as early as four months of age and one of my own females had her first estrus at five months. As a rule, most bitches come into season every six months, thereafter.

Your female will need time to grow and mature before being bred. She must be ready, not only physically, but also emotionally and mentally, for the task of having puppies. I suggest waiting until the second season to breed your bitch. This should allow her to mature without the stress of whelping a litter. Under no circumstances should any bitch, no matter how mature she may appear to be, be bred on her first season.

Most breeders prefer to breed their bitches, for the first time, before they reach the age of four. Certainly, bitches can and do whelp successfully, for the first time, after four. Very often, however, it's more difficult for these older bitches to conceive. Like the very young bitch, the older maiden bitch may encounter difficulties in whelping.

Novices often ask when a bitch is too old for breeding. This is difficult to answer. Breeders frequently continue to breed their bitches into their sixth year. Much depends on the health and condition of the bitch. Frequently, older bitches are less regular in their seasons than younger bitches. You should be aware that older bitches are also more prone to complications during whelping, and a Caesarian may be necessary. Still, if you want one last litter from your fabulous brood bitch and she's still in good condition, you can try.

Most breeders breed their brood bitches one season, then skip the next season. This allows the bitch to recover fully and replenish her resources, in preparation for her next litter. There's nothing that grieves the dog lover quite so much as seeing a bitch bred successively, season after season, until she wears out. If you have a bitch, however, that comes into season every ten months or only once a year, it is permissible to breed her every season. If you feel compelled to breed your bitch on successive seasons, then do allow her to rest on her third heat cycle. Above all, let common sense be your guide. If your brood bitch has a litter of one or two puppies and raises them without difficulty, it might not be too much of a strain to breed on her next season. If, however, she's just finished raising a litter of eight, you're asking a great deal to expect her to raise another litter on her next season.

CONDITIONING THE FUTURE MOM

The best time to begin conditioning the brood bitch is before she's bred. Your best bet for ensuring vigorous, strong puppies and few whelping problems, is to start with a bitch in tip-top condition. Now's the perfect time for a routine veterinary visit. A fecal examination should be done to detect the presence of worms. It's best to have your bitch treated now, before she's bred. You'll also want to be sure she's up-to-date on her yearly vaccinations. Have the vet attend promptly to any vaginal infections. Immediate treatment is in order for any skin conditions that the bitch might transmit to the puppies.

Now is also the time to stop for a moment and take a long look at the future mom's physique. You want to have her in good, hard condition. A flabby, overweight bitch may have difficulty becoming pregnant. She could also encounter whelping difficulties. Place her on a diet before you breed her. Similarly, the thin, underweight bitch is apt to be dragged down by the burden of a litter. Now, not after breeding, is the best time to increase her ration until she achieves ideal weight.

Optimum muscle tone is also important. A bitch whose muscles are in tight, hard condition is likely to have fewer complications. It's usually not difficult to get American Eskimos to exercise. Thankfully, ours is a lively, energetic breed. Still, make sure your bitch gets sufficient exercise. You want her in the peak of condition. Exercise can be especially useful in helping to trim the figure of an overweight bitch. If your American Eskimo bitch would rather relax on the sofa, you'll have to encourage her to exercise. Toss a ball or a frisbee, or take her for a daily walk. While she may be reluctant to exercise on her own, chances are she'll be delighted at the prospect of spending some time

The Standard female, Gr. Ch. 'PR' Denali's Country U-Kay-C, owned by Nancy & Michelle Hofman, shows the alert look so characteristic of the American Eskimo.

with you. She'll feel better and you'll feel more confident in breeding her.

COORDINATING WITH THE STUD DOG OWNER

Contact the owner of the stud you have selected as soon as your bitch begins her season. There's nothing as frustrating, to a stud owner, as receiving a frantic telephone call announcing that a bitch must be bred immediately. Stud dog owners have busy lives, too. Courtesy and thoughtfulness will go a long way toward friendly relations. If you aren't certain of the exact day your bitch's season began, let the stud dog's owner know. He can arrange for you to deliver the bitch a few days early.

UNDERSTANDING YOUR BITCH'S SEASON

It's an aid to breeders to have a basic understanding of their female's heat, or estrus, cycle. If we have a general grasp of how the bitch's body functions during the breeding season, it will make it easier to determine the optimum days for breeding.

Your bitch will be in season for approximately eighteen to twenty-one days. Young bitches may, the first time, have an immature, or incomplete, season of shorter duration. It's easy to miss the first few days of a bitch's season, so close attention is essential. Your first indication that your bitch is in season will likely be the sight of a few drops of blood. You'll also note that her vulva swells, although at this early stage it will feel firm when touched. Some bitches are quite adept at keeping themselves clean. If you suspect that your bitch is in season, you may want to line her kennel, crate or dog bed with a white cloth (an old sheet or white towel is ideal) so that you will be able to confirm your suspicions. Some bitches have a pinkish discharge, but most show bright red blood.

During this first phase, you may notice behavioral changes in your Eskie female. Some bitches become anxious and nervous, while others seem overly affectionate. A bitch may be a bit testy with other females. Don't be surprised if she needs to go out to relieve herself more often than usual. These changes are due to the sudden production of hormones and are quite normal. This first phase of your bitch's season will last approximately one week. You should be aware, however, that all American Eskimo bitches are individuals and many vary from this general guideline.

The second phase of the season is the one that most concerns breeders. It is during this time that the bitch is ready to be bred. By this time, your bitch's vaginal secretion will have changed. Most likely it will become clear or take on a yellowish tinge (breeders often refer to this as "straw-colored"). A light touch of your bitch's vulva, with a piece of toilet paper, will help you to observe this change. If your bitch happens to be one of those who are fastidiously clean, the best time to check is while she's sleeping or the minute she awakens. You'll notice changes in the vulva, too. It will generally show greater swelling and will be softer and almost flabby in nature. The vaginal opening will be more prominent.

The bitch's demeanor will definitely change during the second phase. She'll flirt eagerly with other dogs. If you have her in an enclosure with other bitches, you may find that they are mounting her. Some females become quite brazen in their flirtations. Owners must exercise caution during this phase of the bitch's cycle. Not only is the bitch intensely interested in being bred, but she's extremely enticing to males. The odor of her urine will proclaim to every male that she's available. Indeed, you may find a pack of males camped out

The impressive Gr. Ch. 'PR' Sta La Gi's Satin Doll, owned by Lynne Vickers.

on your front lawn.

Watch closely for your bitch to exhibit the classic telltale sign of breeding readiness...flagging her tail. She will raise her tail and flip it slightly to the side. She'll also elevate her vulva in anticipation. It's best to breed a couple of days after the bitch begins flagging her tail. This is usually on the tenth to the fourteenth day. Treat this on an individual basis. Let the bitch's behavior be your guide. Most breeders breed one day, skip a day, and then repeat the breeding. This increases their chances of selecting a day when the bitch will have ovulated.

The charming 'PR' Winterset's Scarlett, owned by Leroy & Lila Bean, is close to completing her championship.

Don't assume that your bitch's interest in males will diminish after she's been bred. Continue to exercise caution in protecting her. Your bred bitch could still slip out under a fence. Males have been known to go to extraordinary lengths in their efforts to reach a female in season. You must remain vigilant.

During the final phase of your bitch's season, she will no longer be willing to stand for breeding. She may growl or snap at any male who attempts to mount her. Her swelling will diminish and her decreasing discharge will have changed to a dull brown color. Her body is now returning to normal.

As we've said, all Eskie bitches are individuals. Some simply don't follow the commonly accepted rules. There are bitches who routinely have irregular seasons. They may be ready for breeding on the second day of their season. Conversely, one occasionally finds a bitch who should be bred on the sixteenth day. It's very difficult to ascertain the optimum breeding day for such females. You may breed this type of bitch, season after season, without getting her to conceive. You may want to coordinate with your veterinarian. He can perform vaginal smears that will help to pinpoint the ideal day for breeding.

DETERMINING PREGNANCY

The breeding has taken place and now the waiting game begins. If this will be your first litter, you will undoubtedly be anxious. You'll be watching eagerly for any sign that your bitch is pregnant. I'm afraid there is nothing to do but relax. The normal gestation period for dogs in 63 days. However, many females, particulary first time mothers, whelp their litters early.

During the first month of pregnancy, there's virtually no way to tell for certain if your female has conceived. You may be able to detect signs of pregnancy as early as the fourth week. At this stage, you might note a thickening in the width of the loin.

During the fifth week, other changes may become evident. Your bitch may become ravenous, eating her food with great relish. Bitches, particularly those carrying large litters, may look fuller in the belly. It's during the fifth week of pregnancy that you can palpate the bitch in an attempt to feel the developing fetuses. Some breeders are very skilled at palpation, while others just don't have the touch. The same applies to veterinarians. Palpation is effective only in the fifth week for at this stage the fetuses are small, hard and firm. Later, they will be too soft to detect. You should also know that if the bitch is carrying her puppies high up under the ribs, you won't be able to detect them. If you are going to palpate, above all, be gentle. You want to know if there are puppies. The last thing you want to do is harm them. With your thumb and index finger, gently feel along the bitch's abdomen. You are searching for one or

The lovely Ch. 'PR' Hofman's Country Tiara, owned by Catherine Burich & Doreen Rhoan. (!Eddie Rubin photo)

more bumps approximately the size of a hickory nut. Once again, palpation is not foolproof. Don't become discouraged if you can't feel anything.

During the sixth week, you should be able to see definite signs of pregnancy. Your bitch may well have a big belly by this time. Because of the added weight, her topline may begin to sag. Even bitches with strong, sound rears may appear spraddle-legged and cowhocked. You may see that the bitch's nipples are slightly swollen and appear more prominent. The breasts may begin to fill with milk. Remember, however, that your bitch could be carrying a single puppy. Do watch her closely even if you fear that she may not have conceived.

CARING FOR THE MOTHER-TO-BE

Your bitch is now eating for herself and her puppies, and you will have to feed her accordingly. Most breeders have, over the years, developed different diets for use on pregnant bitches. Ask ten different breeders what they feed and you're bound to get ten different answers. This only illustrates that there is no one specific way of feeding that will insure success. There are, however, certain general guidelines that you should follow.

You will, of course, be increasing the amount of food your bitch will receive. Most importantly, you want to increase the quality of her food. Foods high in protein, with a good calcium content, are recommended. The important thing to remember is to make certain that you are using a complete, well-balanced dog ration. Some breeders give a vitamin and mineral supplement, and you may want to ask your veterinarian about this. Be aware that loading her up with additional vitamins is risky, however. Oversupplementation can cause many problems.

During the early stages of her pregnancy, your bitch can continue with her routine exercise. If she has good muscle tone, the whelping will be easier. By the fourth or fifth week, however, it's best to cut down on any really strenuous exercise. Jumping should definitely be curtailed.

Unless absolutely necessary, the bitch should receive no medications or shots during her pregnancy. Some medications can cause birth defects. There have been instances where treatment has been toxic and fatal to the developing fetuses. Unless the condition threatens to endanger the bitch's life, try to delay any medications until after she's whelped her litter.

American Eskimos are, generally, healthy and hardy dogs. They usually experience few problems during their pregnancies. Your best bet for avoiding problems during pregnancy is to begin with a healthy bitch. By conditioning her carefully, insuring correct exercise and feeding her sensibly, you will have prepared her for her job as a mother. As the date she's due to whelp approaches, watch her closely. By being vigilant, you'll be able to see both the physical and behavioral changes, and avoid any problems.

A native Californian and a born Dodger fan!

9

Having Puppies

Delivering a litter of puppies is a natural process for your bitch. We've all heard the stories of bitches that whelped their litters, without assistance, under the porch of an old farm house. There's even the old timer's story of the Foxhound bitch. It seems that the pregnant bitch was part of a pack in hot pursuit of their quarry. During the chase, the bitch stopped, whelped a puppy and cleaned it off. Taking it in her mouth, she rejoined the other pack members, continued the chase and then came home to deliver the rest of her litter.

Natural though it may be, some dogs do need assistance in bringing their puppies into the world. It's advisable for you to be there, just in case there's a problem. American Eskimos are, in general, excellent mothers. Some do, however, need a little help in getting started.

If this is the first time you've attended a mother-to-be, it's natural that you'll be nervous. Just don't let your anxiety consume you. Some bitch owners have panicked at the last moment and rushed the bitch to the veterinarian, so he could do the whelping. The place for the bitch who's beginning labor is at home, unless complications force a trip to the vet. She'll be more relaxed in familiar surroundings.

Your best bet for staying calm is to educate yourself. If you know what to anticipate, the whole experience will seem less frightening to you. By learning as much as possible about what will happen, you'll be able to tell when things are going awry. It's impossible to predict how your bitch will act, particularly if this is her first litter. She may take command of the situation and not need any assistance at all. If she has the situation well in hand, don't interfere.

As the big day approaches, you're likely to become more and more anxious. Take heart for most whelpings go smoothly, just as nature intended. To allay your fears, refer to this chapter and gather all the equipment that you might need. If you have a friend who's a long time breeder, keep the telephone close by. Many an experienced breeder has talked a novice through the process. If you truly fear that there might be a problem, check with your veterinarian. Tell him the date your bitch is due and make sure that he will be there or on call, should you need him during the night.

WHERE TO HAVE THE PUPPIES

Left to her own devices, the bitch will surely choose an inappropriate place to whelp. Stories of bitches who delivered their litters in closets, under the living room sofa, or in the middle of a bed, abound. Give some thought to where you want to house the mom and her litter. You want a place that's free from drafts and reasonably warm. Most importantly, you want a place where mom can feel secure and where she will stay calm. Look for a spot that's away from the hustle and bustle of everyday life. You will also want a location where you can easily glance in and check on her. If you have a guest bedroom, or there's a convenient corner of your bedroom, this may be ideal. It's possible that you'll have several nights when you'll be half-awake, watching the bitch. Having access to a bed, for naps, is handy. If at all possible, you'll want a telephone within easy reach, just in case you do have an emergency.

Your bitch needs to feel protected and secure. This isn't the time to plan a dinner party or issue an invitation to the family to come for a visit. Keep strangers and friends alike away from the bitch. Don't bring people in to see the expectant mother. If there are children in your home, declare the mother-to-be's room strictly off limits. Expectant mothers have been known to act unpredictably.

It's best to provide the bitch with a whelping box. There are many types of boxes, some fancy and some simple. Some breeders elect to use cardboard cartons (those with Standard sized Eskies will find boxes for televisions the appropriate size) for their whelping bitches. These are readily available from grocery or appliance stores. If you decide to go this route, be absolutely sure you

Who wouldn't want to find this in their mailbox?

A beautiful picture. A proud American Eskimo mother with her twenty day old litter of five pups.

know what came in the cartons. You must never use cartons which formerly contained a potentially toxic substance, such as detergents or abrasives. Cardboard cartons don't hold up as well as permanent whelping pens, so you'll need two boxes. One will be used during the actual whelping. You will then transfer mom and her puppies to the other box after the whelping. You'll have to cut an opening in one side of the box, leaving a strip along the bottom about two to three inches high. This will allow mom to get away from the puppies and yet keep them from tumbling out.

Chances are, those with several bitches will opt for permanent whelping boxes. Each breeder seems to come up with a design that suits him. There are, however, several guidelines you should follow. You must be capable of easily sanitizing the whelping box. If you opt for cardboard cartons, these, of course, should be discarded after each use. You'll want to make sure that the mother has an opportunity to get away from the puppies. She must have easy access to them, but be able to escape their constant demands. Some breeders have used a child sized wading pool. You must decide on the bedding to line the whelping box. Some breeders opt for indoor-outdoor carpeting, while others prefer newspaper. If you decide on carpeting, be sure it is secured to the bottom of the box.

It's best to place the mother in the whelping box about a week before she's due. This way she can become accustomed to her new surroundings. Mothers, suddenly placed in a new and strange whelping box, have been known to try relocating their litters to a place of their own choosing. It will hasten her adjustment if you feed her in the box. Encourage her and tell her how good she is for remaining in this strange, new place. By the time she's ready to deliver the litter, she will have settled down and will be comfortable in her new home.

Eskie puppies get into the darndest places. This little tyke has a stuffed armadillo for a playmate.

Most Eskies will be fine in your normal household temperature. Freedom from drafts, however, is essential. You don't want to take a chance on the puppies or the mother being chilled. If you fear that drafts may be a problem, it's a good idea to partially enclose the whelping box, with cardboard or blankets, to keep out the breeze. You may want to provide extra warmth during the whelping and for the first few days. This can be provided with a light bulb or a heating pad on the "low" setting. One caution if you opt for a heating pad. Make certain that the mother cannot get at the electric cord. It's also a good idea to make certain that the heating pad does not cover the entire surface of the whelping pen. Tiny puppies can become overheated and they must have room to move off the heating pad or they will become dehydrated. If your bitch is whelping in winter and there's a heavy wind outside, you may want to place a small heater in the room where she's whelping. This will protect mom and babies until the weather warms again.

WHAT ELSE WILL I NEED?

It's best to collect a few supplies that may come in handy during the whelping. Have a good supply of *newspapers* on hand and a large *garbage bag* for bundling up the soiled papers. It's a good idea to have a *cardboard box* with a heat source. Some mothers become restless while they're whelping. You may want to remove one or more puppies and place them in this box, while she delivers the next addition. You'll want to have several *towels,* for cleaning and rubbing down the puppies. A pair of blunt nose *scissors* is excellent for use in cutting the umbilical cords. You might also prefer to have a *hemostat* on hand, for clamping the cord before you make the cut. Some breeders prefer to use *dental floss* to tie off the cords. It's best, just in case, to have some *Esbilac* or other milk replacer. You'll also want a *baby scale,* for weighing the newborns, and a *pen* and some *paper* for jotting down notes.

YOU AND YOUR VETERINARIAN

We hope that you've already established a close working relationship with your veterinarian. It's reassuring to know that you have someone you can trust, if need be. Don't pester your vet with calls over trivial, insignificant matters as the day of birth approaches. You don't want to gain a reputation as "the boy who cried wolf." Make sure you keep records, such as the days your bitch was bred and the hour she went into labor. These will be helpful to your veterinarian, should treatment be necessary.

Let common sense be your guide in contacting your veterinarian for help. Some vets will tell you not to worry if the bitch hasn't gone into hard labor (had at least one contraction). However, if you honestly believe there's a problem, do make a call. You are within your rights in insisting that the veterinarian meet you at his office. Trust your instincts. While your veterinarian is a well-trained professional, you live with the bitch daily and know her better than anyone else. If you're sure there's a problem, don't hesitate to pick up the phone.

WATCHING FOR THE SIGNS

American Eskimo bitches vary in the warning they will give you as the time of birth approaches. Some exhibit virtually no symptoms. Conversely, other bitches will drive you to distraction several days before the big event. Many bitches become excited, nervous and restless as the big day approaches. There are a few, however, who will remain calm until they go into labor.

One of the early signs to look for is your bitch's attempt to "nest." She'll tear papers frantically, then lie down. In a few minutes she'll be up

A happy, healthy pup, with that glorious, full puppy coat.

again, ripping at the papers with her paws and mouth. She continually rear-ranges the papers to suit herself. Many bitches refuse food, as the time approaches. Some wolf down their food voraciously, only to regurgitate it, afterward. You may notice that your bitch is shivering violently, even though the temperature in the room is very warm. Sometimes you can detect a physical change in your bitch's appearance. She may be carrying her puppies lower and have a "hollow" look in the loin area.

Some bitches, particularly household pets, want you near them at this time. Give your Eskie a few pats of encouragement, try to calm her down and tell her how well she's doing. Stay calm yourself. This period, known as prelabor, may last only an hour or the bitch may carry on like this for a day or more.

TEMPERATURE CAN BE AN INDICATOR

Most breeders will rely on their experience in determining when a bitch is due to whelp. For the beginner, however, charting your bitch's temperature can be helpful. The bitch's temperature will drop shortly before the birth of the puppies. By taking her temperature repeatedly, you'll have advance warning.

The dog's normal temperature is around 101.6 degrees. Individual dogs, however, can vary slightly from the accepted norm. For this reason, it's best to take your bitch's temperature twice a day during the week before she's due to whelp. Take your readings at twelve hour intervals, such as 7:00 a.m. and 7:00 p.m. Avoid taking the reading immediately after your bitch has exercised, as activity may elevate her temperature. Don't be alarmed if her temperature fluctuates slightly during the day. This

Love for sale. Who could resist this little charmer?

After a morning of mischief, this pup relaxes in the shade.

is normal. By taking her temperature in this manner, you'll be establishing a "baseline" that will tell you what is normal for your dog.

When you notice a steep drop in the bitch's temperature, you will want to watch her closely. The temperature will probably drop into the nineties. This is a clear sign that your bitch will whelp some time within the next twenty four hours. If you see no symptoms of labor within a day after the temperature drops, phone your veterinarian. Similarly, if your bitch has not whelped by the 63rd day after breeding, it's best to take her in for a check-up.

LABOR BEGINS

During the first stage of labor, your bitch will become increasingly nervous and uncomfortable. She'll scratch frantically at her papers, lie down and pant for a few seconds and then get up to paw the papers again. She may have a pained look on her face. Don't be alarmed if she whines and trembles. Watch for your bitch to begin licking her vulva. You don't want to interfere with her at this stage. It's best to keep an eye on her from a discreet distance. Don't add to her nervousness.

The beginning stage of labor may last one hour or more. You might try speeding up the process, by letting the bitch outside to relieve herself. Offer her a drink of water. Do, however, exercise caution and keep a close eye on her while she's outside. More than one breeder has discovered that the bitch whelped a puppy outside.

If your bitch remains in this first stage of labor for more than twenty four hours, call your veterinarian. Problems don't usually occur until the bitch has gone into hard labor, but it's best to be on the safe side. Do keep an eye out for

77

Little Winterset Country Lace seems destined for a successful show career. (Doug Kaz photo)

an abnormal discharge. If you see a greenish or black discharge, phone the vet immediately. Excessive bleeding should also be reported promptly to your veterinarian.

HARD LABOR

Hard labor begins when your bitch has her first contraction. The first contractions could be mild and easily missed, so watch closely. You don't want to interfere, but it's best, at this stage, to move closer and keep a steady eye on her. Jot down the time you noticed the first contraction. Don't trust your memory. The contractions will probably increase as your bitch bears down. The contractions may follow one right after the other or there may be an interval of time between them. Much of this depends on where the puppies are, in relation to the birth canal. If this is the first time you've witnessed a bitch in labor, it may look as though she's straining to have a bowel movement. Your bitch will choose a position that's comfortable for her. Some bitches have their puppies lying down and some prefer to stand.

If your bitch is having very hard contractions and she hasn't whelped a puppy in an hour, it's time to call the veterinarian. There may be an overly large puppy that she's unable to expel. It's also possible that a puppy is in an awkward position and jammed at the entrance to the birth canal. In either of these situations, you vet may elect to perform a Caesarian section. If your bitch's hard contractions stop suddenly and don't resume within an hour, call the veterinarian.

THEY'RE HERE!

After one or several hard contractions, a large, black, bubble-like sac will emerge from the vulva. This will probably be the water bag. The appearance of the water bag is an important sign, for it signals the entrance of the first puppy into the birth canal. Be alert, for the puppy usually follows quickly. Occasionally, the water bag will burst in the birth canal, but this is not a cause for alarm.

Most puppies are born head first. The puppy will be encased in a watertight, fluid filled sac. During the months of pregnancy, he has been suspended in this fluid and received oxygen through his umbilical cord. The sac must be torn away from the puppy's head immediately, so that he can breathe air, not fluid, now that the umbilical cord is no longer providing him with oxygen. Make sure the bitch attends to this immediately. If she doesn't, tear the sac away with your fingers. Move quickly. Try to be unobtrusive, so as to avoid upsetting the bitch unnecessarily.

Generally, the bitch will take over. She will pull away and eat the sac. She'll lick the puppy all over, cleaning it and stimulating it. You will be surprised at how roughly the bitch handles the newborn. She may even roll the puppy over, causing it to cry out and thrash around. Don't be alarmed. This is natural and beneficial. As the pup cries out, he's filling his newborn lungs with oxygen.

When the bitch has finished cleaning the puppy, she should attend to the umbilical cord. She will sever it with her teeth. If your bitch fails to cut the cord, you will have to step in and take over this duty. Take a firm hold on the cord, but do not pull it, as

These four month old Miniature pups could melt the hardest of hearts. (Doug Kaz photo)

this will result in an umbilical hernia. Approximately one to two inches from the puppy's belly is where you want to cut the cord. Some breeders prefer to clamp the cord first, with a hemostat. If you opt for this method, leave the clamp in place for a few minutes or until the bleeding subsides. Some breeders also feel it's best to tie the cord. If you want to tie the cord, encircle it with dental floss and make one or two knots. Be sure to cut off all the excess floss. If you don't trim the floss, it will worry the mother and she may tug on it, injuring the puppy. You may also wish to apply a drop of iodine to the remaining cord.

Nine week old Lacy is irresistible.

Be sure to look for the placenta, or afterbirth. This is usually attached to the umbilical cord. The afterbirth is about half the size of the puppy and will resemble a dark piece of liver. Occasionally, the placenta will separate from the puppy and be expelled just after he's born or be pushed out by the emergence of the next puppy.

You'll want to be alert for the appearance of each afterbirth. There will be one for every puppy born. You may want to make a note each time you see one. After the whelping is completed, check your notes. If an afterbirth was not expelled, contact your veterinarian. Retained placentas cause very serious infection and may be fatal to your bitch.

Breeders differ in their opinions as to whether the mother should be allowed to eat the afterbirths. The afterbirth is a rich source of vitamins and nutrients. In the wild, it supplies the mother with nourishment, so that she doesn't have to leave the litter in search of food. Experts also believe that the placenta may stimulate milk production. Unfortunately, consuming the afterbirth has a laxative effect on the bitch and she's apt to have loose stools for a few days. Some breeders remove and discard all afterbirths. Many breeders allow the bitch to eat one afterbirth and remove all subsequent ones. Some breeders believe it's best to allow the bitch to consume as many as she wants. Talk with your veterinarian, or friends who are experienced breeders, to help you decide what to do.

CLEARING THE PUPPY OF FLUID

Once the mother has cleaned up the puppy, you'll want to pick him up and examine him. Some mothers object to this, while others seem to welcome the help. If the mother objects and you feel she's done a good job, you can delay. Rub the puppy vigorously, with a towel, until he's completely dried. Remember, you needn't be gentle. If he hasn't made a sound or if he seems a little sluggish, give a sharp little tug on his tail. This is akin to spanking a newborn human infant on the bottom. He'll cry out and his lungs will fill with oxygen.

Hold the puppy to your ear. If you hear any rasping, rattling or bubbling, the puppy has retained fluid in its lungs. You don't want him to get pneumonia, so it's best to deal with this immediately. You'll want to "swing down" or "shake down" the puppy, as breeders call this technique. While it may sound complicated, once you try it, you'll see how simple it is in reality. Hold the puppy very securely, with his belly resting in your palm. Place the other hand over its back, with the index finger and middle finger behind the puppy's neck and head for support. Stand up straight with your legs approximately shoulder's width apart. Carefully raise the puppy, at arm's length, over your head. Make sure your grip is secure, you don't want to drop him. Swing your arms forcefully in an arc, from over your head to down between your legs. The centrifugal force generated in this maneuver will expel fluid from the puppy's lungs. You'll notice a few bubbles of moisture at the puppy's nose and/or mouth. Wipe these off and repeat the procedure. Place the puppy to your ear once again. If you still hear rasping, repeat the procedure. Continue with this until the puppy's lungs sound clear.

Okay pardners, we're ready to move 'em out.

THE FAMILY GROWS

Bitches may deliver their puppies in rapid succession, or there could be a lengthy break before the next puppy arrives. It will calm the bitch if you leave the puppy with her, until the next contractions begin. Many bitches become restless when the contractions start again. They stand, walk around and tear at the papers. It's best to remove the first puppy, so that mom can concentrate on the task at hand. You wouldn't want her to lie on the pup or inadvertently injure him. Be sure to place him on a heating pad or under a heat lamp.

It's entirely possible that the second puppy may come "breech" or feet first. Such births are fairly common in dogs. Breech puppies may come easily. There is the possibility, however, that the puppy may hang up since the widest part of his body (the shoulders) exits last. Some bitches must give an extra push or two to expel the pup. If the hind legs emerge, but the rest of the pup does not immediately follow, you should help. Grasp the hind legs and hold them securely. If at all possible, leave the sac intact. Pull gently, steadily and very slowly. It's best to pull in time with the mother's contractions. If she isn't bearing down, massage her stomach to stimulate the contractions. Make certain you pull out and down, just as the puppy would come into the world naturally. Once the puppy is out, quickly break the sac, clean and massage the puppy, and swing him down. This is very important, as breech puppies almost always have fluid in their lungs.

Experienced breeders can often successfully turn a puppy which is in an abnormal position inside the mother. They've learned this skill from watching veterinarians, talking with breeders and, most of all, through experience. It's difficult for novices to deal with this type of problem, however. A call to your veterinarian is in order.

Them's mighty big boots to fill for such a small pup, but Stevens' Country Princess looks confident.

HELPING THE PUPPIES TO NURSE

Now that the puppies are here, it's time for them to nurse. Some puppies instinctively hunt for a nipple, almost immediately, while others may not nurse for an hour or more. First time mothers may be uncomfortable having the puppies nurse. Don't worry, with time and patience, the bitch will catch on.

The first feeding is very important. Following birth, the mother produces colostrum. This milky substance contains antibodies that transfer the mother's immunity to the puppies. If a puppy seems reluctant to nurse, you'll have to lend a helping hand. Open the puppy's mouth and place it on a nipple. Squeeze a few drops of milk onto the puppy's tongue. If necessary, support his body while he nurses. Getting a newborn to nurse is sometimes frustrating, but just keep at it. Soon you'll be rewarded by a row of contented little puppies with full tummies.

THE NEW FAMILY

Now that the excitement of whelping is past, you'll be able to settle down and observe mom and her brood. Newborn puppies will nurse and sleep around the clock, during these first few days. You'll be amazed at how quickly they grow. Don't be surprised if the little whelps double in size before your eyes. If the bitch has the situation well in hand, don't interfere. This is not the time for visitors, so don't invite people over to see the babies. Do watch the puppies. You'll be able to determine when something is amiss. Healthy, vital puppies will wriggle and squirm when you pick them up. The weak, listless, limp puppy, who cries incessantly, is a problem. He may not be getting enough milk. It's also best to keep an extra close eye on any very tiny pups in the litter. Make sure that they aren't being pushed off the nipple by their stronger littermates. If necessary, place them on the nipple and make sure they get their fair share.

Make certain the dam is cleaning the puppies. Newborn pups are unable to urinate and defecate on their own for the first few days, and mom must attend to this. She should lick and stimulate them to eliminate. If you fear that the bitch is neglecting this, you'll have to fill in for her. Dip a piece of cotton in warm water and gently rub the pups' private parts.

In the days following the whelping, keep an eye on the mother. It's natural for her to have some discharge, usually reddish brown in color. She may also continue to bleed. If you notice excessive bleeding, particularly if it's bright red blood, contact your veterinarian. Be alert for

Muffin, owned by Richard & Judy Bobick, takes times out for a nap.

any sign of a greenish discharge. This type of discharge usually means that a placenta has been retained and could spell serious trouble, if not treated promptly. If the mother seems weak or listless, has an elevated temperature, or goes into convulsions, take her immediately to the veterinarian.

Your bitch will probably have a voracious appetite. Continue feeding her as you did when she was pregnant. Allow her to consume as much food as she wishes. Also, be certain that the bitch is supplied with plenty of clean water. You'll be surprised at how much she drinks. This is normal, don't be alarmed.

The puppies' eyes will open at about two weeks of age. It's fascinating to watch them discover their new world. By two or three weeks, they'll be staggering onto their feet and trying to take their first faltering steps. In another short week, they'll be walking without difficulty. However, if you've had a litter with only one puppy, it may take him a little longer to begin walking. You'll want to clip back the puppies' toenails at this stage. The tips can be taken off with a pair of scissors or a human nail clipper. Be careful to remove only the white tip and avoid cutting into the pink vein, known as the "quick."

WEANING TIME

Weaning should begin at three to four weeks of age. Some mothers grow fussy during the third week and spend more time away from the puppies. Conversely, other mothers will stay with their pups well into the sixth week, even allowing them to nurse once the sharp milk teeth have emerged. Generally, mothers with small litters will continue to nurse for a longer period.

Most American Eskimo puppies are avid eaters and your litter will

A pair of Eskies get their first taste of puppy food.

probably take less than a week to wean. I start by giving the pups two feedings a day. I begin with a pabulum type human baby cereal mixed with warm water. Mixed in equal parts with the water, this has a very sloppy, gruel-like

84

What a beautiful baby! This is little Country's Kaz E-Z Money, owned by Esperanza & Doug Kaz.

appearance. Pour the food into a shallow dish or onto a plate. A pie pan is ideal. Stick the puppies' noses in the pan, or place some food on your fingers and allow them to lick it off. Don't be surprised if your puppies are messy. They'll take a few bites of the food, walk in it, fall in it and, generally have a wonderful time making absolute messes of themselves. When they lose interest in the food, return mom to them. She'll finish up the remainder of the meal, including what's on the pups.

Once the puppies are eating the cereal well, you can begin introducing them to solid food. Buy some puppy kibble and soak it in warm water, until it swells up and becomes soft. Mix this with a small amount of the cereal. As the puppies become familiar with this, decrease the cereal until they are eating kibble alone. A small amount of cottage cheese or canned meat can be added to the kibble. Some breeders begin their puppies on milk, but very often this causes loose stools. Be sure to provide clean water for the pups. After you have the pups eating successfully, you can gradually begin decreasing the amount of food the mother is receiving.

Puppies have small stomachs, so it is important to feed small amounts frequently. Generally, I give my puppies four meals a day until they reach three months of age. At this stage, they are usually cut back to three feedings per day. I continue this thrice daily feeding schedule, until the puppy has reached eight months of age. From eight months to two years, I feed the dog twice daily. Some breeders, however, pare the dog back to one meal a day at one year of age.

SOCIALIZATION

As the pups grow, you'll want to give them attention. After the first week or so, you'll probably pick them up, cuddle them and love them, while mom is out exercising. Puppies need love to grow into stable adults with charming personalities. You may want to expose them to household sounds. The television, radio and vacuum cleaner, as well as the clatter of pots and pans, and the ringing of the telephone, may startle and frighten them at first, but they'll quickly adjust.

If the weather is warm, pups can be taken out at about five weeks of age. Be sure, however, that they have access to the shade. You may want to provide them with toys. An old work glove or discarded sock makes an excellent and inexpensive play toy. While they love squeaky toys, it's best not to allow them to play with these. They could tear apart the toy and accidentally swallow the squeaker.

VACCINATIONS

Your puppy will gradually lose the immunity he obtained from his mother. There's no precise date when this will occur. It's best to check with your vet to see when he wishes to start the immunization program. It will probably be at six to eight weeks of age. Generally, puppy vaccinations are given as a series of two or three shots. Since there's no way to tell exactly when the mother's immunity will end, the multiple shots will ensure that the puppy is adequately protected. Don't stint or think you can save money by skipping the shots. The cost of vaccination is very small, compared to the cost of treating a dog who has contracted distemper, hepatitis, leptospirosis or parvovirus.

Your puppies are now well on their way to becoming well adjusted adult American Eskimos. More than likely, you'll decide to keep at least one of the litter. With a little luck, it could become your first homebred champion. The other puppies will go to loving homes. Be sure to check back, periodically, with their new owners. Go to see the puppy or request a photo. By keeping in touch with the people who purchase your pups, you'll be better able to evaluate the litter. This will be of great help to you in planning your next breeding.

10

Showing Your American Eskimo

Exhibiting purebred dogs is one of the most popular family sports in America. It is an ideal group activity, in which everyone can participate. The whole family can be involved with raising, conditioning, training, grooming, feeding and showing just one dog.

While showing dogs is a fascinating sport, knowing what to do, ahead of time, can relieve a lot of anxiety. Showing a dog is not complicated, but it is a "learning" experience and should be enjoyable to both young and old. New dog owners, unfamiliar with basic ring procedure, may easily become discouraged and confused. If their dogs are inadequately groomed or trained, they may become frustrated and disillusioned. Sometimes the other exhibitors, at the show, are too busy to offer the guidance and advice the novice needs. In this chapter, I will attempt to cover the basic information you will need to participate in U.K.C. shows. Don't expect to learn everything at once. Go to the shows and enjoy yourself. You will learn as you go along. Not everyone has the necessary skill to become a successful exhibitor. Some people display a greater degree of natural ability than others. Don't let this intimidate you. You will never know, unless you try. Many average handlers, with good dogs, win at shows and, with proper preparation, you stand an excellent chance.

Everyone loves their American Eskimo and thinks their dog is smarter and more beautiful than any other. At shows, however, you must remember that there can only be one Best of Show winner on a given day. Each and every exhibitor paid his entry fee and wants to win. Therefore, we must create an atmosphere of fun and togetherness at a dog show. This way, we will enjoy ourselves, whether we win or lose. After all these years, I do not consider myself an exceptional handler, but I like attending shows and handling dogs. I love all the fun and camaraderie that develops among show people. On the other hand, my husband is an excellent handler, but he does not enjoy showing as much as I do. He much prefers the creative challenge of breeding dogs, in an effort to improve the breed. It's his form of artistic self expression.

UNDERSTANDING U.K.C. SHOWS

People attending their first dog show are often confused and bewildered by the entire proceeding. United Kennel Club shows, however, are well organized and follow a logical pattern. American Eskimos are entered in classes based on their size and age on the day of the show. Miniatures are judged before Standards, and males are always judged before females. By keeping these simple rules in mind, you will be able to follow the judging sequence.

American Eskimos are shown in two divisions, according to their height. To qualify for the *Miniature* class, males must stand at least 12 inches at the withers (the highest point of the shoulder) and may not exceed 15 inches. Females must be at least 11 inches

The impressive Standard male Gr. Ch. 'PR' Maxwell's Illamar Hofman. This lovely show dog was bred by Nancy & Darrel Hofman and is owned by Tom Maxwell.

tall and may extend up to and including 14 inches. Miniature male puppies are allowed to enter as long as they measure at least 11 inches and female pups must stand at least 10 inches high. *Standard* sized American Eskimo males must be over 15 inches, at the withers, and up to 19 inches. Standard females must stand over 14 inches but may not exceed 18 inches.

The first class that will be judged is the Miniature *Puppy Class* for males that are six months to one year of age. Next comes the Miniature *Junior Class* for males. Entered in this class will be males that are one to two years of age. The Miniature *Senior Class* for males consists of dogs that are at least two years of age, but less than three years. The last males to be judged are those entered in the Miniature *Veteran's Class*. These are males over three years of age. After the Veteran's Class has been judged, the winners of the Puppy, Junior, Senior and Veteran's Classes will be brought into the ring, to compete against one

Showing dogs can be a great hobby, as Lila & Leroy Bean have discovered. Pictured is their Ch. 'PR' Tsa-La-Gi Billy Jack.

another. The judge will select one male as *Best Minature Male of Show*. The same classes, in the same order and with the same age requirements, are then judged for Miniature American Eskimo females. After the class judging, the female winners of all the classes will be brought into the ring, and the judge will select the *Best Miniature Female of Show*.

At the completion of the Miniature judging, the Standard sized American Eskimos will enter the ring. Once again, males will be judged before females and the classes have the same age breakdowns listed above. A *Best Standard Male of Show* and a *Best Standard Female of Show* will be selected. The judge will then call the Best Miniature Male and the Best Standard Male into the ring, to compete against each other. The winner is declared the *Best Male of Show*. The Best Miniature Female and the Best Standard Female next enter the ring, and the *Best Female of Show* is selected. The Best Male of Show and the Best Female of Show are required to enter the ring for a final time. The judge will select one of these Eskies as the *Best of Show* winner.

Most American Eskimo shows include a *Champion of Champions Class,* which is judged after the Best of Show has been selected. Both Miniature and Standard males and females compete against each other in this class, which consists of dogs who have already earned their U.K.C. championship titles. Some American Eskimo shows also feature a *Grand Champions Class.* To qualify for this class, males and females must have already earned the U.K.C. Grand Championship title. Champion of Champions and Grand Champions classes usually require dogs to be entered, by mail, in advance.

American Eskimo shows usually offer some non-licensed classes, too. *Novice Puppy* classes are frequently offered. Some clubs divide this class into two age divisions (2-4 months and 4-6 months). This class enables breeders to gain valuable ring exposure and experience for their pups. *Junior Handling* or *Junior Showmanship* classes are also commonly offered by show giving clubs. This class allows youngsters to participate and gain ring experience. The Junior handler is judged on his ability, not on the dog's conformation. Judges take time to offer tips to the youngsters and may quiz them on dog care or points in the standard. For children, emphasis should be placed on having fun.

Part of the fun of attending dog shows is meeting and travelling together with friends who share a love for showing dogs.

HOW CHAMPIONSHIPS ARE EARNED

The United Kennel Club awards *Champion* (abbreviated CH.) and *Grand Champion* (or GR. CH.) titles. Points toward a championship are earned by winning first place in the Puppy, Junior, Senior or Veteran's classes. In both Miniatures and Standards, the winners of each of these classes receive five points toward their U.K.C. championships. The Best Miniature and Best Standard Males of Show and the Best Miniature and Best Standard Females of Show receive an additional eight points toward their titles. The Best Male and Best Female of Show are awarded an extra ten points for their achievements. Finally, the dog selected as the Best of Show receives an additional twelve points. Thus, a minature male that won first place in the Junior Class, for example, and then went on to be judged Best Miniature Male, Best Male of Show and then Best of Show, would earn a total of 35 points toward his championship. This is the maximum number of points that can be awarded at any one show. In order to earn a championship, an American Eskimo must accumulate a total of 100 points. Furthermore, these points must have been earned under at least three different licensed judges. For an American Eskimo to complete the championship requirements, the dog must also have been awarded at least one Best Male or Best Female enroute to the title. Dogs who began their show careers as Miniatures and then matured into Standards, keep any points garnered in the Miniature classes.

A well posed dog. This is the Standard male Gr. Ch. 'PR' Country's Lucky Diamond, owned by Sandy Tocco.

The Grand Championship title can be earned by American Eskimos who have already completed and been confirmed as U.K.C. Champions. In order to earn a Grand Championship, dogs must compete in the Champion of Champions class. They must win the Champion of Champions class in at least three shows under three different licensed judges.

SHOW TRAINING

At dog shows, the rank novice with his first dog can compete side by side with the person who has finished many champions. If his dog is best, chances

90

are the beginner will win. In order to compete successfully, however, your dog must have some show training. Without this basic schooling, he is apt to lose despite his superior quality. While this may seem unfair, it is actually quite reasonable. A judge has only a limited amount of time, in the ring, to assess the quality of the dogs exhibited. If a dog refuses to stand still so that he can be adequately examined or balks at moving around the ring, the judge has a difficult time seeing his virtues. This is particularly true in large classes, where there are many top quality dogs from which the judge can make his selection. Show training is not difficult and, with a little practice, your dog will be ready for the big time.

WORKING WITH PUPPIES

You can begin training your young pup as soon as he's mastered walking on a lead. Working with young pups can be great fun. It can also, at times, be extremely frustrating. Puppies have short attention spans and you must keep this in mind. Make the training fun. If your puppy is more interested in playing, it's best not to fight him. Let him play and return to the training later. Limit your training sessions to five minutes. In training pups, you must have patience. Refrain from working with the puppy if you are tired or irritable. Screaming, yelling or hitting can only damage the relationship you are trying to build.

As a rule, American Eskimos do not approach strangers readily. Therefore, as soon as your puppy has had his shots, you will want to get him out in public. Take him to shopping centers and public parks, where he will come in contact with many people. He will soon learn to cope with the strange surroundings, noises, distractions and crowds. Eskie puppies are tremendously cute, and you and your pup are sure to be approached by strangers. Encourage them to talk to and pet the puppy. Such training will do nothing

The outstanding winner National Gr. Ch. 'PR' Smith's Arctic Snow, owned by Betty & Clarence Smith. Arctic was the first Grand Champion in Michigan and is the sire of champions.

to alter your dog's guardian instincts. Instead, it will build self confidence and your dog will feel comfortable in any situation.

Puppies learn at their own pace. Some learn very rapidly, while others take a little longer. I've had one puppy that learned to pose beautifully after only three five minute sessions. Most, however, take longer. Don't try to push your puppy too fast. Overtraining can break his spirit and thwart his enthusiasm for showing. Remember to praise your puppy often.

POSING YOUR DOG

You will need to purchase a "show lead" for your dog. Most owners use one-piece, lightweight show leads. These can be obtained at pet stores, from supply catalogs and at some shows. It's best to use the show lead only when training or actually showing your dog. When you want to take him for a walk, switch to a regular leash. This way, the dog will quickly learn that, when you put the show lead on, he is expected to settle down and work.

Dogs are "stacked" or "posed" in the show ring. This is also sometimes referred to as "setting up" your dog. You need to train your dog to stack perfectly and remain motionless while the judge examines him and evaluates his conformation. Teaching your dog to stand four-square in the show ring is really a simple task, which can be accomplished with a minimum of training. Most American Eskimos are self-stacking and will strike a naturally attractive pose. Often, however, they may have a foot or two out of position. It will help if you learn to adjust the dog's stance. You don't want your Eskie to look as though he has faults which aren't really there.

In working with your Eskie, remember to keep the dog on your left. Tell your dog to "heel," and move him around in an imaginary circle. Come to a stop and tell your dog to "stand" and then to "stay." He will soon learn to stop immediately. If your dog starts to sit, take him forward a couple of steps and repeat the stand/stay command. If he once again tries to sit, slide your left foot very gently, under him. This will keep all but the most determined dogs from sitting.

Take a moment to look at your dog. Is his stance square? His front legs should be placed beneath his shoulders and facing straight forward. His hindlegs should be slightly farther apart than the front and his hocks should be vertical. His topline should appear strong and level. At rest, your American Eskimo may carry his tail down. Many breeders, however, prefer to see the tail carried over the back.

If your dog is not standing correctly, you will want to reposition him. If his front is out of line, there are two ways to correct the stance. Place your hand under his chest and lift his front an inch or so into the air. Slowly lower him.

A lovely show dog, owned by Dean & Gloria McKee. The Standard male 'PR' Cascade Shasta Sno is close to finishing his championship.

The lovely Gr. Ch. 'PR' Hofman's Lil' Bit Country, owned by Nancy & Darrel Hofman.

If your dog has a naturally straight front, he will be standing correctly. If only one foot is out of position, you may wish to correct only that leg. If it's the dog's left foot, reach over his shoulder and grasp the leg at or just below the elbow. Shift the dog's weight onto the other foot and place the errant foot correctly.

Before repositioning the hind feet, you need to hold your dog's head up. This is done either by using the show lead or placing your hand under the dog's muzzle. If the dog's left leg is out of position, reach beneath the stomach and gently grasp the stifle. Shift the dog's weight off the foot and place it in the proper position. The right rear leg is positioned in an identical manner, but, of course, there's no need to reach under the belly.

Males should become accustomed to having their testicles touched. In the ring, the judge must check to make certain that both testicles are present. Run your hand down the dog's back and then gently reach underneath and touch the testicles. After a few sessions, your dog will not object to this.

Take a final look at the topline. If it is sagging, gently prod or tickle your dog's stomach. Run your hand gently down the dog's back and, if he's dropped his tail, place it in proper position. Most Eskies hold their tails properly, but if your dog tends to drop his, hold it in position. A tickle on the underside of the tail's base will usually help to keep the tail up. Once again, tell your dog to stand and stay. Try to get the dog to hold this pose for a few seconds at first. You'll want to gradually extend the length of time he can stand posed.

In the show ring, you will be required to show your dog's bite to the judge. Most dogs object to this initially, but your dog will soon learn to accept this. To show the bite, place your right hand under the dog's jaw and your left

A well posed Miniature female, Ch. 'PR' Maxwell's Sonseearay, owned by Tom & Ruth Maxwell.

hand on top of his muzzle. Pull down the lower lip at the same time you bring up the upper lip. What the judge wants to see is the dog's incisors (his front teeth).

You want to learn to pose your dog quickly and efficiently. As you gain experience, you will learn to stack the dog with a minimum of fussing. It can sometimes be difficult for the novice to tell if he has his dog properly positioned. You might want to try stacking your dog in front of a mirror. This way you will immediately be able to see when you've struck the ideal pose. You'll also be able to experiment with posing the dog in various ways, to determine what's best for your dog.

GAITING YOUR DOG

Your Eskie will be gaited, or moved, in the show ring. This helps the judge to discover faults that may not be apparent when the dog is standing still. There is nothing quite so beautiful as seeing an alert American Eskimo gait effortlessly around a ring. At shows, dogs are moved in a counter-clockwise circle about the ring. They will also be gaited individually. Proper movement is very important in our breed, so it will pay to practice gaiting your dog at home.

Always hold the show lead in your left hand. Fold or ball up any excess lead in the palm of your hand. Held properly, you will be able to fully control your dog on a show lead. When moving your dog, you can adjust the tension on the leash simply by raising or lowering your arm, or by feeding out or gathering up the lead. Move your dog in an imaginary circle. If he begins to lag behind you, give a quick jerk or two on the lead and he will speed up. If the dog moves away from you, a little

Junior Showmanship can be great fun for youngsters.

94

jerk will bring him back in line. Likewise, if he veers toward you and begins to crowd in too close, an outward jerk will straighten him out.

It will take a little practice to determine the ideal speed at which to move your dog. Eskies should be moved at a brisk, animated trot. You don't want to run full out, as though you and your dog were in a race. Neither do you want to walk along, taking small mincing steps. You want to move at a speed which allows your dog to hit an easy, free moving stride. To determine the correct speed for your dog, it is best to enlist the help of a family member or friend. Have them watch from the side as you move the dog. Tell them to let you know when the dog moves the best. You might also want to watch, yourself, as someone else moves the dog. With a little experience, you'll be able to tell when your dog is moving at his best speed.

The extraordinary Standard male, Gr. Ch. 'PR'Tinker's Toybear, owned by Carolyn Kane. (Eddie Rubin photo)

Gaiting should be included in your practice sessions. Drill your dog in gaiting both in a circle and in a straight line. It's best to prepare the dog for any eventuality that may occur at a show. You will want to practice both indoors and out. Accustom him to a variety of surfaces. He should learn to move willingly, whether he is on a floor, cement, grass or bare ground.

POLISHING THE ACT

In the show ring, you want your American Eskimo to perform with zest and animation. There's nothing more irresistible than a lovely Eskie, with eyes sparkling, ears up and head held high. While the judge will be comparing the dogs' conformation, in a close decision, that extra spark might give the decision to your dog. In U.K.C. show rings, baiting, or attracting the dog's attention by the use of food, squeakers, keys or some other device, is not permitted. A handler is allowed to speak to his dog or to snap his fingers to attract the dog's attention. American Eskimo judges, however, often use attention getting

The impressive Gr. Ch. 'PR' Muffin's Casper, owned by Suzanne Truitt. (Eddie Rubin photo)

devices, to help them see the dog's animation and expression. They may use keys, a squeaky toy or a piece of cellophane, such as a candy wrapper. Many judges also drop a pair of keys on the floor. This aids them in determining that the dog has good hearing and is not deaf. If you wish to practice at home, occasionally, with some of these devices, you can. Beware, however, of overdoing it. If the dog gets too used to hearing keys jangling or a squeaking noise, he may not respond in the show ring.

THE VALUE OF PRAISE

Be sure to give your American Eskimo plenty of praise while working with him. Eskies are very intelligent and they respond well to training. It is never necessary to handle your dog roughly or to hit him. Always remember that this breed will work for the sheer joy and fullfillment of pleasing you. The Eskie wants your approval. Patience, persistence and training will pay off, and you will have a beautifully behaved show dog, who performs like a champ.

LOCATING A SHOW

Now that your dog is trained for the ring, you'll be anxious to show him. How do you locate a UKC sponsored show for American Eskimos? Subscribe to the U.K.C. publication, *Bloodlines*. All American Eskimo shows are advertised in this magazine. One of the best ways to learn about local events is to join a breed club (the addresses of American Eskimo clubs are listed in the appendix). By joining a club, you will be able to meet people you have something in common with...you all love American Eskimos. In addition to learning about shows, you will make friends and learn more about the breed.

The show advertisements, printed in *Bloodlines,* include much information. The name of the club and the date of the show will be listed. Pay attention to the amount of the entry fee and, especially, the time deadline for the closing of entries. Entries will not be accepted after this hour. The advertisement will include the name of the judge and may specify an alternative judge. There will also be additional helpful information, such as directions to the show grounds and the names of motels or hotels close to the show site. The ad will tell you whether food will be available or whether you should plan on bringing lunch from home. The names and phone numbers of one or two persons will be listed, in case you need more information.

PACKING YOUR BAGS

A day or two before the show, you will want to gather all the supplies and equipment you intend to take with you. Until you become a seasoned show hand, you may want to make a list, so you won't forget anything. To enter your dog, you will need to show your U.K.C. papers. Take your dog's registration papers and pedigree or the newly introduced E-Z Entry Card. You will also need your Eskies rabies certificate and, for some shows, a health certificate. Be sure to take along the directions to the show and the address of the motel or campground where you will be staying. Pack an extra show lead, in case you misplace yours or it breaks. I always bring along a can of disinfectant spray. Gather together all your grooming equipment. Be sure to bring a gallon of water from home, and your dog's food and water dishes. If the show is being held in the summer, freeze water in milk cartons. These can be placed in the dog's kennel, to keep him cool and, once melted, will supplement the water supply. To cope with an unforseen emergency, you may want to bring along a first-aid kit. Paper towels, plastic garbage bags and moistened towellettes will also come in handy.

If the show is being held outdoors, you may wish to bring along lawn chairs, a blanket or a rug. If food is not available at the show site, pack an ice chest. Include sodas, food and munchies for your dog. Be sure to pack a raincoat, in case there's a downpour.

What an exciting day for any breeder! Ch. 'PR' Hofman's Sabrina Royale and Gr. Ch. 'PR' Maxwell's Illamar Hofman complete their championships on the same day.

97

You might also want to include a change of clothing, in the event you should get drenched. A large fluffy towel or two will come in handy, if you have to dry your Eskie.

PROPER SHOW RING ATTIRE

You want to wear comfortable clothing that's appropriate for the season. Your clothing need not be dressy, but it should be in good taste. Avoid tight fitting clothes that may restrict your movement. Women should refrain from wearing low cut blouses. Very full skirts are also inappropriate, since the material can catch under your shoe as you bend down to pose the dog. Such skirts also make a swooshing noise, which is distracting to the dogs. Shoes are very important. They should be comfortable and practical. High heels or sandals are never appropriate for a ring appearance. I've seen more than one person twist an ankle, or fall, because of improper footware. Heavy charm bracelets that clank will distract your dog and the judge. Likewise, long heavy necklaces, that brush against your dog when you pose him, should be left at home. It's also best to prepare for emergencies. Be sure to take a raincoat and, if the weather is cool, take along a warm jacket.

It is best to wear dark clothes when you are showing your American Eskimo. The Eskie's white coat will contrast best against a dark background. Black, blue and red outfits show off the Eskie's coat to its most beautiful appearance. Your choice of color will be particularly important to you if your dog wins. Photos will be taken of the winning dogs and you will often look back at those photos with great pride and satisfaction. I have one lovely picture of one of my champion bitches. Unfortunately, I wore a white jacket that day and the dog's head does not stand out at all well against that background. The photo was taken the day she completed her championship.

Gr. Ch. 'PR' Sassi's Crystal Misty shows the happy alert look that judges like to see in the show ring. Owners are Lila & Leroy Bean.

It was a very special day and I would have liked a wonderful photo to capture the moment.

BEFORE YOU GO IN THE RING

Let your dog relax before you go into the show ring. It's a good idea to walk him so that he can eliminate, if need be. Permit him a small drink of water, but don't let him drink too much, or he's apt to have a "pot bellied" look.

If you aren't in the first class, be sure to observe the judging. It can be very valuable to see how the judge organizes his ring. You will see if he prefers to gait the dogs around the ring immediately or if he examines the dogs before moving them. Perhaps the judge examines all the dogs before gaiting any of them individually. Or he may examine each dog, gait him and then proceed to the next dog. By paying close attention, you will know what to expect when it's your turn to go into the ring.

IN THE RING

The big day has finally arrived, and you and your dog are ready for your show ring debut. Chances are you will have butterflies in your stomach and your knees may knock. It's quite likely that your dog can sense your nervousness and will be tense, too. Take a big breath and try to relax. Remember, everyone else in the ring was a beginner at one time.

Each judge has his own procedure for conducting the judging in his ring. While there may be variations, I will describe the most commonly followed pattern, here. When your class is called into the ring, enter promptly. Don't make the other exhibitors wait for you. Most judges signal everyone to go counterclockwise around the ring. This allows the dogs to settle down and gives the judge an

A big win for one of Charlene Dunnigan's American Eskimos. This is Gr. Ch. 'PR' Sierrs'a Snow Shadow.

A wonderful example of superb Eskie movement. Here Rosemary Stevens moves her Gr. Ch. 'PR' Steven's Toybear Apollo. (Holloway photo)

overall impression of the class. Move your dog out at a brisk trot, but remember this isn't a race. If your dog starts to run, give a quick jerk on the lead to get him under control. You want the judge to see your dog moving at the pace that's best for him. Don't run into or crowd the dog in front of you. Neither should you move so slowly that the dogs behind you jam up. After one or two circuits of the ring, the judge will indicate (usually by holding his hand up) that he wants the dogs to stop.

The first handler in line should stop his dog. If your dog stops in an awkward position, you will need to adjust his stance. Either take a step or two forward until the dog is standing squarely or reach down and place him in the proper position. Unless instructed otherwise, remain in the same order you entered the ring.

The judge will now begin his individual examinations of the dogs. Most judges wisely approach from the dog's front and often extend a hand so the dog can sniff it. He will ask you to show him the dog's bite. The judge will begin by examining your American Eskimo's head. He will be looking at the shape, length and width of the head and the placement of the ears.

The judge will then look over your Eskie's front and shoulders. You don't want to get in his way and obstruct him. Stand inconspicuously to the side while the judge is examining the dog. Each judge has his own procedure for evaluating the front and shoulders. The judge will feel to determine the dog's shoulder layback. Some will lift the legs and release them, seeing how they drop naturally into place.

Next, the judge will look at the dog from the side. He may span his hands over the dog's ribs to judge their spring. He will probably run his hand down the dog's back and may apply slight pressure, to insure that the topline is strong and straight. He will then move to the dog's rear. As the judge moves to the rear, you should move to the head to steady the dog. The judge will examine the hind legs and may reset the rear himself. If your American Eskimo is a male, the judge will feel to make sure that both testicles are present. If your dog has dropped his tail, the judge may lift it to the proper position.

When he's completed the examination, the judge may step back to take a final look at your dog. If your Eskie has moved out of position, quickly place him in the proper stance. When individual examinations are completed, the judge will want to see you move your dog. He will ask you to gait in one of several patterns. If you have been paying attention, you will know what to expect. If yours is the first dog to be judged, and you are not sure of the judge's instructions, by all means ask for clarification. Check your show lead, to make sure it's in the proper position, and then gait your dog as the judge requested. This is an important exercise, so gait your dog at his best speed. If your dog breaks into a gallop or acts up, stop. Give your dog a jerk to get his attention and then begin again. Remember to keep your dog between you and the judge. As you are returning, keep an eye on the judge. The judge may hold up his hand, indicating that he wants you to stop a few feet in front of him. Slow down and bring your dog to a stop. Try to maneuver him into correct position, but do not manually position him.

Return to the line of dogs as the judge continues his individual examinations. Make sure you keep an eye on the judge. If you are competing in a very large class, you may allow your dog to relax. When the judge begins examining the last dog, it's time to pose your dog. The judge may walk up and down the line, giving the dogs a final look. In a large class, he may pull out one or two dogs and ask them to move again.

At this point, the judge will likely have decided on the winners. He will ask all the dogs to circle the ring again. Even if you think you have lost, don't let up. Judges have been known to change their minds on the final go-around. As you circle the ring, the judge will usually call out and point to the winners, "One, two, three." If you are one of the lucky winners, go to the appropriate placement marker. You

A smiling American Eskimo with her trophies. Gr. Ch. 'PR' Stevens' Country Princess, owned by Sandy Tocco, was the nation's top Eskie in 1984.

101

will then receive your ribbons and any trophies for your class. If you placed first in your class, don't leave the show grounds. You will be called back into the ring for further competition.

BE A GOOD SPORT

You should always act in a courteous, considerate fashion at a dog show. It's very bad form to interfere with other dogs, while you are in the ring. Don't allow your dog to lunge or growl at other dogs. Your dog may be excused from the ring if he becomes a nuisance. Pay attention while you are in the ring. Don't indulge in conversations with those standing at ringside. There will be plenty of time for that later. While you may talk to other handlers in the ring, keep your voice low and don't break the judge's concentration. Remember, the judge is in the ring to do a job. Don't engage him in conversation. Some judges will barely speak with exhibitors during judging. If the judge realizes that you are a novice, he may say a few words, in an attempt to calm and relax you. This does not mean that he's inviting you to have a lengthy conversation. It is inappropriate to tell the judge about your dog's show record or any of his previous wins. The judge will not be persuaded if you tell him, "My dog needs only one more win to finish his championship."

If you would like to know the judge's opinion of your dog, ask him after your class has been judged. Most judges will take a few minutes to evaluate the dog for you. The dogs faults and virtues will be fresh in his mind. The judge is under no obligation to discuss your dog with you and may politely refrain from doing so.

Not everyone can win and you must learn to take both the wins and losses with equal grace. Learn to control your emotions. Don't jump wildly about, screaming and yelling, if you win. This will only distract the dogs. Likewise, don't storm out of the ring, stamping your feet, if you should lose. There will be another show on another day and your dog will have another chance to win. Thank the judge graciously for the ribbon he gives you. Be sure to sincerely congratulate the winner. Extend your hand or give the person a hug. By acting courteously, you will help keep dog showing a fun sport.

11

Training Your American Eskimo

American Eskimos have long been star performers in UKC obedience trials. It's no wonder. This breed combines inherent intelligence with a strong desire to please. Furthermore, Eskies are a relatively easy breed to train. Even novices, who've never before trained a dog, find their Eskies easy to work with. Many owners find great satisfaction in presenting their American Eskimos in the obedience ring. In general, Eskies are happy, enthusiastic workers. Their eyes sparkle and their tails wag as they perform the exercises. While you may not be interested in gaining an obedience title or winning trophies, your Eskie will still benefit from basic obedience training.

Let's look at some of the day-to-day, practical applications of training. Have you ever watched someone taking an unruly dog for a walk? The dog drags the poor owner along, tugging and lunging, until it appears that the person's arm will be yanked from the socket. Sometimes the dog wraps the leash around his owner's legs, tripping him. Walking such a dog quickly becomes a chore, rather than an enjoyable outing. A properly trained dog walks quietly at his owner's side, even on a busy street. How many times have you opened a door or gate, only to have your Eskie run out? If your dog knows the "stay" command, he'll remain in place, when the door or gate is opened. It's also very convenient to have your dog trained to "come" on command. Surely, you've watched someone attempt to chase and corner an Eskie. The dog runs wildly about, darting here and there, just out of reach. With growing frustration and rising blood pressure, the owner chases the dog. By the time the dog is finally captured, the Eskie is exhausted and the owner is fuming. How much nicer to tell the dog to "come" and have him respond immediately. Should your dog escape from your yard, obedience training might well save his life. If your dog hightails it for the street, a "down" command will cause him to drop immediately. This response might prevent him from ending up under the wheels of a car.

In addition to the practical advantages of owning a trained dog, there are other benefits. Obedience training is an ideal way to form a close bond with your dog. No other activity develops such an intimate rapport between owner and dog. You and your Eskie will learn to function as a team. Most American Eskimos are eager to please and they genuinely enjoy learning. Training will constructively channel your dog's abundant energy. Furthermore, trained dogs are generally happy dogs. They are a pleasure to take out in public and they help to give people a positive impression of the breed.

A BRIEF INTRODUCTION TO TRAINING

Obedience training your dog is not difficult. Dog clubs, in many cities, hold weekly training classes, during which the owner is taught to train his dog. There are also numerous books which give step-by-step instructions for training. By devoting a few minutes each day to working with your dog, you can have a well-trained companion in short order. Even if you have no desire to participate in obedience competition, your dog will benefit from learning the basic commands. While we cannot include in-depth training instructions here, we will give you an idea of how to teach your dog the basics.

For basic training, your dog will need a suitable collar. A slip collar (often called a "choke" chain) is best. For American Eskimos a medium link chain, which slides easily, is preferred. It's important that the collar fit properly. When the collar is pulled snugly against the dog's neck, there should be about three inches of spare collar. Contrary to its name, the choke collar is not

The proper way to put on a choke chain. The Eskie model is Country's Kaz E-Z Money, owned by Doug Kaz.

meant to choke a dog. Used properly, it applies quick pressure to the dog's neck and is immediately released. Such collars are not cruel or harmful. You'll also need a leash. A five or six-foot leather or nylon web leash is best. Chain leads are hard on the hands and will telegraph any corrections to the dog.

Every dog should learn the five rudimentary exercises that are the basis for all obedience training. The dog should be able to "sit" on command. He should walk at your side, or "heel," on and off the leash. He should be taught to drop, or "down," when ordered. He should

These puppies, bred by obedience enthusiast Donna Blews, are starting their obedience careers at an early age.

also learn to "stay" when so instructed. Finally, he should "come" when called. We'll describe for you, briefly, the basic methods of teaching each of these five essentials. Regrettably, space allows us to give only the briefest of instructions.

Heeling

There are a few basics to remember when teaching your dog to "heel." The dog is always on the handler's left side. This is referred to as the "heel" position. In heeling, the dog should walk quietly at your left side. His shoulder should be in line with your leg. He should not forge out in front of you, nor should he lag behind. Your dog should be attentive and learn to keep up with any changes in your pace. If you speed up or slow down, the dog should, too. If you make a turn or a turn around, the dog should turn with you.

Place the dog in a sitting position, at your left side. Take a step forward with your left foot. Simultaneously, give a little jerk on the collar and command, "Sam, heel." Remember, this is an active command, in which the dog will be moving. Therefore, use his name first. Start by walking in a straight line or a circle. If the dog starts to forge ahead or move off to the side, give a quick jerk and repeat the command, "Sam, heel." A small jerk, which brings the dog back in position, is all that is necessary. If needed, several successive jerks may be used, but you do not want to drag the dog. You may want to talk to your dog enthusiastically while he's heeling. This will keep the dog's focus on you. Remember, you want the training to be fun, not drudgery. Now, halt. Tell your dog to "sit." Be ready to reach down and help guide the dog into an automatic sit. Anytime you stop, your dog should routinely sit. Keep heeling with your dog, giving small jerks whenever he veers from heel position.

Next, you'll want to teach your dog to do an about turn. When executing an about turn, you want to either pivot or take small mincing steps. You should always reverse your direction by turning to the right. Your Eskie may continue

Gr. Ch. U-UD, U-CDX, U-CD 'PR' Northern Lights Nokomis - TT, SKC CD, owned by Donna Blews, demonstrates the broad jump.

on in the direction he was going when you made your turn. As you begin your turn, give your dog a quick jerk and reiterate the command, "Sam, heel."

Your dog should also be taught to make right and left turns. Your turns should be abrupt and sharp in angle. Right turns are seldom a problem. Simply, give the dog the heel command and a short jerk when beginning your turn. Left hand turns are a little trickier. Early in the training, use the lead to let the dog know what is coming. Nudge or brush the dog with you leg, when making the turn. If the dog starts to move away, a small jerk will bring him back to position.

Your dog has now learned the basics of heeling. Eventually, you'll want to try heeling off leash with him. Don't be too quick to try your dog off leash, however. Starting him too soon may set back the training. Make sure your dog is working perfectly on lead and paying close attention to you, before you try working off leash.

The Sit

To teach the sit, place your dog on a leash. With the dog at your left side, give him the command to "sit." Hold the leash in your right hand. Pull straight up on the leash, while applying downward pressure to the dog's haunches with your left hand. Repeat the command so that the dog associates it with the action. Take your hand away. The dog should remain in a sitting position. Beginning dogs will likely stand up. Don't be annoyed. Place your dog back in a sitting position and tell him, once again, to "sit." When he has remained in place for a few seconds, praise him. Be sure to tell your dog how wonderful he is for obeying you.

The Down

There are two ways to teach the "down" and both are effective. With your dog in a sitting position, give him the hand signal and the command, "down." You can give a small downward jerk with the leash and pull the dog down. Or, with one hand, pull your dog's front legs so they are extended out in front of him. With the other hand, press down on the dog's shoulders. As soon as your dog is down, tell him "down, good." Now, remove your hands from the dog. If he stays where he is, all is well. It's likely, however, that he will sit up again. Repeat the procedure. You may want to pet the dog while repeating, "down, good." If the dog starts to rise while you're stroking him, tell him "no," place your hand on his withers and press down, repeating "down, good." This will keep him in place. When your dog stays for a few seconds, praise him. American Eskimos often feel vulnerable in the "down" position, so it may take several sessions to teach your dog this command. Be persistent and your dog will soon learn what you want.

The Stay

This is one of the most important of the obedience commands and one that will come in handy in everyday life. Have your dog on the leash and place him in a sitting position. Stand in front of your dog. Hold the leash, partially folded, in your left hand. Hold the leash tautly, slightly behind your Eskie's head. Give the dog the "stay" signal and the voice command. With the taut leash, you'll be able to keep your dog in place should he try to move. If he

The thrill of victory! A proud U-CDX, U-CD Ch. 'PR' Tocco's Mister Ruffy, owned by Sandy Tocco, thinks obedience is fun.

107

doesn't try to get up, take a couple of steps backward and let the leash go slack. The dog may get up and try to follow you. Tell him "no," put him back in position and tell him, again, to "stay." Gradually, you will increase your distance from the dog until you are at the end of the leash. You will also want to lengthen the amount of time you spend away from your dog. The "stay" should be used with both the "sit" and "down" commands. Be sure to praise your dog when he stays successfully.

The Recall

Place your dog in the "sit" position. Tell him to "stay." Walk to the end of the leash and call your dog. You'll note that in the other exercises, you have given the dog a single word command. However, since you want the dog to move in this exercise, you'll use his name first. In an excited voice, say, "Sam, come." Keep the tone of your voice light and enthusiastic. Praise the dog as he moves toward you. Most dogs will immediately come to you. Use both hands to reel in the leash, as he comes to you, so that he won't get tangled in it. Tell your dog to "sit" when he is in front of you. If your dog does not respond to the "come" command, give a jerk and reel him to you with the leash. If your dog seems lackadaisical about coming, give the leash a quick jerk and, with small steps, run backwards. This usually prompts the dog to run to you. As before, have the dog sit. Your dog has now learned to "come" on command and much praise is due him.

Unfortunately, the above discussion gives only the briefest possible treatment of the basics. We strongly encourage you to sign up your Eskie for

U-CDX, U-CD 'PR' Kaz Northern Bandit, owned by Doug & Esperanza Kaz, leaps the broad jump.

108

obedience classes. If none are available in your area, purchase a book on obedience and start at home. Both you and your American Eskimo will benefit from the experience.

One final note regarding obedience training. Praise and correction are the basics for all training. Most American Eskimos are eager to please. You will build on this by giving your dog profuse praise, whenever he does anything right.

U-CDX, U-CD Ch. 'PR' Tocco's Mister Ruffy takes the high jump. Owner Sandy Tocco.

Always try to be consistent in everything you do. Variations in the way you give commands, or corrections, will confuse your dog and delay the training process. Keep the training light and make it fun. Your voice should radiate enthusiasm and delight. Never, under any circumstances, lose your temper. This can be very difficult to carry out. There will be times when you will become frustrated and angry. You'll be tempted to scream and yell, and may want to hit your dog. Don't! Hang up the leash and begin again when you've calmed down. Just don't give up. Patience and consistency are important in all types of training.

OBEDIENCE COMPETITION

The United Kennel Club offers three obedience titles to dogs who demonstrate their proficiency in trials. These are the Companion Dog degree (U-CD), the Companion Dog Excellent title (U-CDX) and the Utility Dog degree (U-UD). A specified series of exercises is required for each competitive level. A perfect score is 200 points, and a dog must earn at least 170 points to qualify for a "leg" toward his degree. Furthermore, the dog must score at least half the points allotted to each exercise to earn a qualifying score. An American Eskimo must demonstrate his proficiency by earning three legs, in order to qualify for his title. These scores must be awarded under at least two different licensed obedience judges. Jumping is required in each level of U.K.C. obedience competition. American Eskimos are measured and required to jump the height of their withers.

U-CDX, U-CD 'PR' Kaz Northern Bandit retrieves the dumbbell over the high jump. Bandit is owned by Doug & Esperanza Kaz.

As we've said, many American Eskimos have proved to be outstanding obedience performers. Since this breed is so good at obedience, most American Eskimo clubs host obedience classes along with their shows. Watching Eskies work can be a delight, especially in the advanced classes. As an added bonus, dogs that are spayed or neutered, while not eligible for the show ring, may compete in Obedience Trials. A complete set of the U.K.C.'s obedience regulations are printed annually in *Bloodlines*. You can obtain the regulations by writing to the U.K.C.

12

A Tribute to the American Eskimo

An Eskimo is "not just a dog"
    He is the personification of forgiveness to man.
He is the symbol of what man should be without his vices.
    He has courage without man's vindictiveness.
He loves and is loved and shows his love
    In every way, his own way,
Simply and without fanfare
    For his love comes from deep within his heart.

Mrs. Don Catlin

Our Name, Our Heritage

You call us a "Spitz?" Oh, come now please.
We have our own name, so let's rest at ease.
Our name is AMERICAN, thru and thru,
And the ESKIMO shows just what we can do,
When we have a boy and that boy has a sled,
We are out in the snow till it's time for bed.
You call us a "Spitz?" Oh no, not that,
And we read in *Bloodlines* most breeders stand pat
On our very own name and a proud name, too,
It does justice to us and also to you.
Our eyes are coal black, lips and noses are too.
Our heads are wedge-shaped. No, that's nothing new.
Our tail's long and bushy; our four feet are flat
With very long hair twixt the pads and the fat.
Our muscular shoulders are strong, as you know,
And our chests deep and broad as befit Eskimos.
We're proud of our heritage,
Proud of our looks,
Proud that our owners discuss us in books.
Proud to be able to ride in a car,
And proud to stand guard if it be near or far.
If you look for a pet,
Don't forget these few lines,
From an Eskimo breeder
With a U.K.C. mind

Mrs. Don Catlin

112

Softness Is...

Do you know what softness is?
The downy feel of a
      puppy just whelped...
The watching of new born puppies as
      they struggle for life...
The fear that they won't respond after
      the sacs removed...
The tiny toes that wiggle back
      and forth
The pinkness that slowly turns to a
      startling black...
The love you feel inside to see how
      wonderfully God works.

To touch and feel and hold a tiny
      mass of fur...
A wiggly body, a tiny mouth...
To watch each day a new experience...
The growth and development of
      beautifully formed little bodies.
A twitch here, a twitch there,
      a flicker, a movement...
Eight little bodies of excitment....
The wonder of the mad rush to the
      "dinner table"...
The amazement of knowing they cannot see
      They cannot hear...
But through some sort of lovely
      reasoning, they know...

Softness, Softness...
The wonder of eight tiny
      American Eskimos!

Nancy J. Hofman

113

Those Nervous Owners Sez They

This obedience school is really fun,
But the whole thing **could** be overdone.
Don't they know what we do, we do to please?
We know what the trainer says, we don't freeze.

We understand English and what to do.
So why the fuss. Getting all in a stew
Isn't going to help us, and it won't help you.

So let's keep our cool and let's find the pace,
We're not going to fall down flat on our face,
No we're not going to bring you any disgrace.

We **all** do well, that's a well known fact.
We don't use diplomacy and we don't use tact,
We just act natural, so why don't you?
So we'll get our trophy and ribbons too.

Mrs. Don Catlin

A Puppy's Prayer

Please God of puppies, take care of me.
When I find my new home that's readied for me.
Don't let them maul me and toss me around.
I'm just a baby.

When I go to a place that is new and strange,
I try to be good, and I'm easily trained.
If you'll have have patience and treat me fair,
You will never know how I might despair.
I'm just a baby.

I will love you all if you give me a chance.
Just let me rest when I'm tired and tense.
Feed me often and plenty of milk
And encourage me when I tend to wilt.
I'm just a baby.

In the weeks that go by, you will see such a change.
I will grow big and strong and will guard my domain.
Take care of the children and grown-ups too.
And prove, with fierce loyalty, thanks to you
I'm no longer a baby.

Mrs. Don Catlin

To Give

A little blonde boy and a little white pup,
There's not too much difference in bringing them up.
They both have to learn the meaning of "No."
They both must be taught the right way to go.
They both have to give and they both have to take,
They both have to realize their own mistake.

In the years to come, both have to grow up,
The boy to a man, the dog, not a pup.
They find that the world is a good place to live
If they think back and remember that little word "Give."
Such a small little word, but is it so rare?
"For the gift without the giver is bare."

Mrs. Don Catlin

My Little Kitiza

She has the brightest eyes and such a devilish smile
Fluffy white hair and tail wagging all the while
Whenever I have to leave and get ready to go
She dances behind, swaying lovingly to and fro
I lay asleep at night and she's loyally by my side
She walks down the street next to me and fills me with pride
Sometimes she pounds on my shoulder when I nap
Doesn't wake me with a rude yap
Saying I know you're tired, but I've got my pride
It's that time when I have to go outside
It's hard to understand the love I feel for this American Eskimo
A loving companion and a champion at every show!
How I wish people would express their love like this American
    Eskimo
Then they would see and understand the joy I know
I've met a lot of people and they've usually let me down
Ruined my days and made me frown
But my lovely, little Kitiza always makes me smile
Gives me a reason for staying around awhile
So if you want to be happy, listen to what I know
Go out and buy yourself a loving American Eskimo

Doreen Rhoan

Growing Up

We open our eyes when we're ten days old,
We don't see too much and we're not too bold,
But there's nothing wrong with our ears and our nose
That a bowl of warm Pablum won't soon disclose.

We like our warm Pablum and wade right in,
More gets on the outside the gets on the in.
Then we each get a bath and we go to sleep,
We don't even take time to count puppies or sheep.

Another day and we learn some more,
Who moved that paper on the floor???
And who put that puddle beside the door?
And what's that thing around our necks?
They call it a collar. Ye gods, what's next?

Now, Pablum is just for the little pups.
We're big guys now, so more cups.
We have our own dish, but it won't stand still,
It's all over the floor, and it sometimes spills.

Next comes a thing that they call a lead,
That's tied on that collar, and that's not feed.
And first we walk on a little short chain,
To struggle and lunge is all in vain.

We walk with that thing just ten minutes a day,
So we won't get too tired and there's still time for play.
And soon we are walking out on the street
Close to the side of our mistress. That's neat.

We feel we know something and somebody cares,
Which means a whole lot on just how we fare.
Our aim is to please, and we do that with joy.
We're much more obedient than some girls and boys.

Mrs. Don Catlin

True Love

You call me a "thing," but I'll tell you, Lee,
There's nothing else in this world that I'd rather be
Than a little white dog belonging to you,
To live in your house, to do as you do.

I know I'm a "thing," but the world is mine.
I've found me a boy, a boy who is kind,
A boy who cares what happens to me,
A boy I depend on and who depends on me.

It isn't always a beautiful coat,
"Eight inches each side" or you "miss the boat."
It's what's in a doggy heart that counts,
And that really makes these doggy points mount.

A boy and a dog. They're hard to beat.
When you see them walking down the street
You see love and devotion, loyalty, all,
They're meant for each other and they both walk so tall.

Mrs. Don Catlin

Vacation Time

We went fishing, the bosses and me,
To a mile high lake amidst tall pine trees,
It was the very first time I had seen a boat,
And at the sound of that motor, I nearly choked.

I looked in the water and what did I see,
Another Eskimo looking at me.
His ears stood up just like mine,
And his nose and his eyes were just the same kind.

I wasn't about to let things go,
And let a strange dog, whether friend or foe,
Spoil a perfectly wonderful ride in a boat,
And to catch **my** fish and to get **my** goat.

I bristled right up and started to growl,
As the boss caught a fish and I swallowed that growl.
And the big boss roared a few choice words,
So I kind of figured I'd be seen, not heard.

We had a perfectly wonderful day,
In the cool mountain valley, but we had to pay
When we came down that mountain,
Boy, was it hot...110 by the "heat o'clock."

I'll dream all night how I loved my day
Curled up in the boat, and I must say
That up there, where it's quiet and peaceful and cool
You're closer to something akin to rare jewels,
You know God made man and animals, too,
And the lake and the pines and the beautiful view.

Mrs. Don Catlin

What Do You Dream?

What are you dreaming, my baby pup
When you turn and you twist and you sound so gruff,
Or is it a gain in your tummy so small,
Or is it either one at all?

What do you dream, my baby pup,
When I hold you and stroke you...my bundle of fluff,
Are you far away in the frozen North
Pulling your pack sled back and forth?

Or are you high in a penthouse tall,
Where you can look down and watch things so small,
And I'll bet you are proud to have people know
In the Northland, in a penthouse, pet or show
That you're quite at home wherever you are,
And your black eyes sparkle like northern stars.

Mrs. Don Catlin

This Worming Deal

Do you know what she gave me, my "human" mummy?
A great big pill to put in my tummy.
Do you think that that was a nice thing to do?
It sure got me in an awful stew.

First, she gave me a nice little piece of meat,
All chopped up fine. A regular treat.
I gobbled it down. Boy, was it good.
It was twenty-four hours since I'd had any food.

Then she gave me some more, and I ate that too.
Then do you know what I thought I'd do?
I thought I would take a nice little nap,
But something happened. I felt a rap.
It seemed to come from my little old tummy.
You needn't start laughing, cause this isn't funny.

It rapped again, and I thought, Oh Gee,
Just what on earth is this going to be?
What was in that meat that I thought was so rare,
Do you 'spose my "Mummy" didn't play fair?

It rapped again, and I sat down quick.
The lights went out, *and was I sick.*
My tummy throbbed and my head did too,
And I didn't know what in the world to do.

My "Mummy" came over and held me tight,
And said, "Poor baby, you'll be alright."
But I didn't care then if I would be or not.
My feet were cold and my tongue was hot.

But it's all over now, and the worms and me
Mutually agreed to part company.
But next time, by gosh, when I'm offered raw meat,
I'll be a little bit more discreet.

Mrs. Don Catlin

Broken Bones and All

This broken leg deal is a pretty good thing.
The "hurt" soon gets over, then this cast brings
Friends that I never knew I had.
Boy friends and girl friends, Moms and Dads.

It happened out in my own back yard,
I was on my long chair, and I was off guard.
The other dogs stood in their kennel runs,
Not too well pleased at *my* having fun.

A big black Lab from across the street
Came tearing over...(he's just a dead beat)
He was taught by his boys to grab anything small,
My front paw was there, I went down for a fall.

There was startled silence, then you should have heard
My own dogs to the rescue. An explosion occurred.
A vocal one, but the Lab ran home,
But there I was with two broken bones.

It didn't hurt then, it was numb all over,
And I limped toward my pen...my fun all over
My mistress came out and covered me up.
We ended up at the local vets
With a cast on my leg, thanks to big black Jett.

I kind of feel sorry for big black Jett,
He has had no training, no shots, no pets
I think that he senses, and probably knows
That his 'cross the street neighbors, the White Eskimos
Have the warmth, love and security he falls to get,
And that's half what's the matter with big black Jett.

Pretty soon it is back to the runs for me,
I've been kept in the house to heal properly.
You'd never know now that I'd had a cast,
Those weeks in the house have surely gone fast.

Mrs. Don Catlin

Index